All Change

MEMORIES OF A RAILWAY ENTHUSIAST

BOB BRUETON

BREWIN BOOKS

First published by
Brewin Books Ltd, 56 Alcester Road,
Studley, Warwickshire B80 7LG in 2008
www.brewinbooks.com

ISBN: 978-1-85858-426-3

A Cataloguing in Publication Record
for this title is available from the British Library.

Typeset in Baskerville
Printed in Great Britain by
The Alden Press.

Front cover: Top – Britannia 70023 Venus in spotless condition awaits her next duty code 102. Bottom – Fowler 'Crab' 2-6-0 42765 at Bewdley Severn Valley Railway awaiting departure for Kidderminster at the enthusiasts weekend September 2004.

Rear cover: The End – or is it? Preserved railways have kept steam alive. Ex GWR 7802 Bradley Manor calls at Arley station Severn Valley Railway on a warm summer afternoon Friday 15th August 2008. The atmosphere is all there – semaphore signals, milk churns, tool shed, signalbox, well kept station and wisps of steam. The author was on volunteer station duty on this day. Photo by Viv Brueton.

All Change

T- Barbara
Hope you enjoy
the book
Best Wishes
Bob.

8F 'Consol' with a long coal train at Bromford Bridge 1961.

CONTENTS

ABOUT THE AUTHOR

Bob Brueton entered this world at the Sorrento Maternity hospital in Moseley Birmingham on 12th October 1943. His parents had both been working hard in the war effort. His mother Ann Elizabeth had worked on a press in a munitions factory. His father John Richard was working in a rolling mill, his work exempted him from the armed services. He did however serve in the Home Guard and was a St. John's first aider.

Bob spent the first four years of his life in a back to back house in Cooksey Rd, Small Heath. The house was a stone's throw in one direction from the Great Western Railway and in the opposite direction from Birmingham City Football Club. Railways and football have been a major interest of Bob's throughout most of his life!

Various events led him to become interested in railways to such an extent that it became a lifelong hobby. In pursuit of his hobby Bob has travelled throughout Britain witnessing at first hand the widely differing areas, cultures and changes through the years. He made many friends, some for life, got into a few adventures and mishaps and overcame many hardships. Organising outings and travelling has always been of benefit, he got top marks in 'O' level Geography and still arranges many outings in his job as a community worker!

Bob has many memories of life in the 50s and 60s growing up in a small Victorian house in what is now described as an inner

The author Bob Brueton ready for work on the Severn Valley Railway as a ticket inspector.

city area and moving out to the suburbs in his late teens to a modern council housing estate.

Bob has had a wide and varied career from mechanical engineer, teacher and now a community centre manager.

When steam finished on BR in 1968 he retained an interest in railways but other commitments, not least a wife and family became important. However 'rails' modern, model and preserved are still important. He actively works on the Severn Valley Railway as a volunteer and is a member of the Birmingham Model Railway Club.

A word of caution – there are instances in this book which relate to misdemeanours including trespass and fare dodging. Bob would warn against these practices, with today's faster, quieter and more efficient railways the risks are greater and the penalties are higher!

Enjoy and support modern, heritage and preserved railways.

FOR THE RECORD

Memory is a wonderful thing but it does need a nudge sometimes. I am pleased that I kept most of my trainspotting notebooks and my Ian Allan ABC's. I also hung onto a range of tickets, magazines and brochures all of which have helped when compiling this book.

I am also pleased that in 1959 I purchased my first camera a Kodak 44a very cheap and very simple. However I took many photographs, not all of great quality, but sufficient to evoke memories, some are included in this book. I regret not graduating to a better camera earlier than 1968 just too late to capture the end of steam.

Thanks to Roy Baker, Brian Dunckley and my sister Sally for photos and memories, Alex Scott for advice and my family Viv, Dawn and Steve for tolerating me, encouraging me and typing up drafts.

I am also grateful to other people's memories reminding me of things I had forgotten. I hope that readers of this book will have their memories jogged and gain pleasure from it.

Chapter 1

THE BEGINNINGS

Maybe it was something to do with living the first few years of my life near to the Great Western Railway in Small Heath, an inner city suburb of Birmingham. I certainly have vague recollections of the sights and sounds of a railway, particularly the clattering of shunting and the continual drifting smoke and grime (a lot of this was probably from houses and factories).

Maybe it was the annual summer holiday to Rhyl, always by train, my parents didn't ever own a car. I recall exciting journeys, large crowds, sitting on a suitcase, noise, smoke, steam, smells, smuts in my eyes!

Maybe it was shopping trips to the centre of Birmingham, the tantalising glimpse from Station Street into the gloomy depths of New Street station, steam, smoke, noise, smells – especially fish!

All of these and more probably sparked my interest in railways which has remained a lifelong interest, or is it an obsession?

However, I think my 'real' introduction to railways began when at the age of 8 (1951) my father considered me old enough to 'go fishing' with him. These angling trips were always on a Saturday and seemed to start in the middle of the night. Frantic preparations were made on Friday evening, sorting rods and lines, packing sandwiches and drinks, storing maggots, worms and groundbait securely. Then it was early to bed, only to lie awake with excitement and be woken up again at 5.30am! A hurried breakfast (who feels hungry at 5.30am?), quick "swill" (brummie wash) and off.

The number 8 tram stop on Alum Rock Rd was only half a mile away but with all the heavy gear it seemed much further. I was always amazed at how many people were up and about and the queue at the tram stop was lengthy, we sometimes had to wait while two or three trams filled before we boarded one. More excitement! I used to try and stand behind the driver with his brass control lever, clanking his bell, watching cyclists and the occasional car dodging out of the way. Lurching over the points at the Gate,

1

across Saltley viaduct, up Great Lister Street and into the City Centre. All this was soon to change and it was the number 14 bus we caught, not so exciting but a lot more comfortable!

The tram terminated in Union Street and the 'bus in the Old Square outside the giant Lewis's department store. Depending on our destination we would either walk down Corporation Street to the grimy entrance arches of New Street station or through the wonderful Great Western Arcade to the splendid façade of Snow Hill station. We never used Moor Street and in fact my father travelled from Moor Street for the first time in 1980!

My father's favourite fishing spot was on the Worcester canal near Stoke Works and luckily for me when I started 'spotting' it was near to a point where the Birmingham to Bristol main line crossed the canal. Stoke Works station was situated where the main line to Bristol and the line to Droitwich and Worcester diverge. The salt works dominated the scene with the large

Probably where my interest really began. This is the exact spot where my father took me on his fishing trips. The bridge carries the Birmingham to Bristol main line over the Worcester canal between Stoke Prior and Hanbury.

salt pans and mounds of dried salt. To get there we had to catch a Worcester stopping train from New Street. The train departures were displayed on a large roller blind in a glass fronted case facing New Street, the blind was rotated regularly using winding handles (unlike today's computerised displays).

Tickets were obtained in the gloomy entrance hall followed by a long walk across the wooden causeway to platform 10 or 11 on the Midland side with its great arched roof. As we crossed the causeway there were steps down to the platforms and each stairway at its entrance had an arch and a large lamp. As each was passed, glimpses of coaches, engines, trolleys, pigeon baskets and lots of people could be seen through the murk of smoke, steam and filtering daylight. The smell and the atmosphere always excited me, a mixture of gas, fish, smoke and steam.

Our train was usually a short local hauled, I discovered later, by a Fowler 4F 'Duck 6' or a Deeley 2P 4-4-0. There were several interesting features to see on the way, the murky tunnels on leaving New Street, the canal running alongside the line, the Cadbury's chocolate factory at Bournville with its gardens and its own steam engines, the huge Austin Motor works at Longbridge also with its own steam engines.

The absolute highlight however was the Lickey Incline, one of the steepest railway inclines in Britain (1 in 37). There was the pungent smell of hot brakes as the train was held in rein ready for its stop at Bromsgrove at the bottom of the 2 mile long steep gradient. There was always a lot to see; the brakeman pinning down brakes on wagons at the top of the incline, passing a train going uphill with a crescendo of noise from the train engine and the banking engine(s). Bromsgrove had its own small engine shed for the banking engines. There was always a freight train waiting to tackle the climb, a line of banking engines waiting to assist. The return journey was even better, I tried to position myself in the rear window of the rear coach so I could be a few feet away from the smokebox door of the banking engine. What a thrill! The noise, the steam, the smoke, the heat. Then over the top at Blackwell and the banker would ease off and recede into the distance as our train continued on its way to New Street.

On arrival at Stoke Works my father was not content to fish near the station but walked seemingly miles along the towpath to his 'favourite spot'. It certainly was a lovely place, fields each side, a farm with cows and sheep, dragonflies, water skaters, plenty of fish and a steam train every few minutes! I remember on the way back we called at the pub in Stoke Works, Dad for his pint, me for my lemonade before the journey home.

I have been back recently (2004) for a "reminisce". Nothing has really changed, the trees are taller, the trains are all diesels but the farm is still there with its cows and sheep. There was a man fishing in the same spot, a young lad was with him, was he a trainspotter?

Another fishing and trainspotting paradise was Worcester. In those days it was a major rail centre with services to London including the 'Cathedrals Express', Wolverhampton via Kidderminster, Hereford, Birmingham, Bristol and the branches to Bromyard and Shrewsbury via the Severn Valley. It had large engine sheds and a loco works. My fondest and earliest memory is racing up the wooden stairs at Foregate Street Station just in time to see the polished brass nameplate 'Saint David' go past That was the only 'Saint' class engine I ever saw.

At the tender age of eight I had become fascinated by railways, excited and thrilled being on or near a train but had not yet started 'trainspotting'. The breakthrough into collecting numbers came as a result of two clearly remembered events. Firstly, my friends had told me about this 'smashing place' where they had seen trains with names like 'Samson, Novelty and Scottish Horse'. A request to my Mother to visit this 'smashing place' was turned down flat. Secondly, she did promise to take me to see the trains next time we went shopping to 'town' – this being the centre of Birmingham.

Visits to 'town' were not frequent but were always exciting. Once again it meant catching the tram or bus (not as early in the morning as the fishing trips!) and usually a walk down to the Bull Ring market area. What memories of the markets! There was a steep slope down from High Street past the statue of Nelson to St. Martins Church. Seemingly all the way down this slope were barrow boys, flower sellers, people selling from a suitcase, noise, smells, hustle, jostle, people of all shapes and sizes. It was exciting and frightening, I remember holding my Mum's hand very tight. There was a man who did tricks with cups and a ball, a man with a monkey (I don't recall a barrel organ), a very tall man with a stripey suit, a black man with curly hair. There was also a woman who called out in a loud voice "andy carriers, andy carriers" with an armful of brown carrier paper bags.

One of my uncles was a barrow boy and my mum always went to see him. I remember all the fruit piled up on his barrow and as he served a customer sometimes an apple or orange would roll off into the road. A lad who helped him would pick it up and put it into a wooden box on the barrow, this was the specs box for damaged fruit to be sold off cheaply. I was often sent shopping in Alum Rock Road for 'a bag of specs', my parents were not well off and this was a way of making the money go further.

Alongside the street market was the imposing fish and meat market with its arched entrance reached via a flight of steps. I was endlessly fascinated by the fish laid out on marble slabs, the ice and the water running off into little culverts. There was also the macabre sight of dead animals – rabbits, pheasants and chickens hanging from the stalls. Just to the right of the markets steps, tucked into the building, was a stall that sold mushroom stalks, the heads of the mushrooms must have been sold to wealthier customers elsewhere, I have never found out! My father loved these stalks and my mother would buy a bagful, they would later be cooked and the tasty mushroom 'gravy' mopped up with a chunk of bread – delicious!

Behind the market hall was New Street Station with Queen's Drive dividing the old Midland and LNWR sides. This was the first time I had entered the station this way and as we turned onto the LNWR side (it would have been platform 6) an engine went past with the evocative name 'Zanzibar' Jubilee 45638 – my first ever written down number – my first 'trainspot'. I can clearly remember two other named engines on that day – 'Derbyshire Yeomanry' Patriot 45509 and 'The Lancer' Royal Scot 46155. I also recall a tank engine with some wagons at the end of platform 6 – this must have been the station pilot. I transferred the numbers into a notebook until I was able to afford an Ian Allan ABC.

Once the bug had bitten my mother had to be persuaded to allow me to go trainspotting locally, I had friends who went and so long as she knew where I was and how long I would be how could I come to harm? Thinking back now, I am certain that if she had known some of the hazardous situations we got into, my trainspotting would have ended there and then! Part of persuading her was achieved by doing extra jobs including cleaning and shopping.

Shopping in the early 1950s was not a 'one stop' trip to a giant hypermarket but a series of separate visits to baker, butcher, grocer, greengrocer, chemist etc. on the Alum Rock Rd. Money was tight and food rationing was still in force, I remember the coupons to be exchanged for a slice of cheese cut off a block with a wire and wrapped in greaseproof paper. I also remember sugar weighed out and put into blue bags, soap in blocks – no fancy wrappings, pork ribs from the butcher for a stew. The Co-op grocers fascinated me with its system of overhead wires along which ran metal containers holding money. These were sent by the assistant to a central cashier in a 'booth' and returned with the change and receipt. I also have imprinted in my memory my mom's Co-op 'divi' number – 4426. At a certain time of year a dividend was paid related to purchases, a welcome bonus to a hard up family. I recall another method of sending cash to a central point in a department store in the city, I can't recall which store. Money was put into a round cylinder which was then put into a tube and with a loud hiss it was gone! It returned a few minutes later with a hiss and a plop as it fell into a wire container. I think it was vacuum operated, probably similar to Brunel's atmospheric railway in Devon!

The cleaning was hard graft – no modern appliances like vacuum cleaners. I cleaned the linoleum floor covering with a bucket of soapy water and a cloth. I scrubbed the front door step with a brush (the door step was an indication of how clean the house was!) The kitchen sink, cooker and floor were also cleaned with considerable 'elbow grease'. Then there was the window cleaning, dusting and general tidying up. I earned my trips out!

I have two other memories of visits to "town". One was for the annual students' carnival procession around the city centre streets. There were two processions, one in the afternoon and one in the evening. These were awe inspiring events with decorated lorries and people in costumes but most impressive were the handheld flaming torches which illuminated the scene in the evening. The second was Christmas at the giant Lewis's department store. Sometime in early December "Santa" would arrive in a horsedrawn sleigh accompanied by his companion "Uncle Holly". Vast crowds would be there to greet him. He would then take up "residence" in his grotto on the sixth floor of the store until Christmas. I remember long queues up six flights of stairs and around the outside of the building to see him. Magic!

The 'persuading' worked and I was soon allowed to go trainspotting with my friends within a couple of miles of home. These local trips are described in more detail in chapter 3.

All of this was happening in my childhood years and it seems appropriate at this point to move briefly away from railways and recapture memories of growing up in the 50s and 60s.

Chapter 2

GROWING UP IN THE 50s AND 60s

My first three years of life 1943–46 were spent in a back to back house in Small Heath, what were later known as 'slums'. Outside toilet and wash (brew) house were shared, no garden just a cobbled courtyard in which were a row of dustbins and 'pigbins' for waste. My only memories of the house are a coal fire with black grate, oven either side, hanging kettle and pot. There was a school almost next door and I recall watching through the window at children on their way (the school was Cooksey Rd Junior).

In 1946 we moved to the comparative luxury of a two up, two down Victorian house no. 12 Mendip Avenue, Alum Rock. Sole use of an outside toilet, own small garden, own dustbin, fireplace in every room, own coalshed! Still no bathroom just a tiny kitchen with a crock sink for washing (cold water only), and an ancient gas cooker. All the windows were sash with a system of ropes and pulleys and big gaps for the wind to come through. Newspaper and old rags were used to plug these gaps. The 2 up 2 down were rooms about 10 feet square, back living room, front parlour and two bedrooms. The kitchen was about 6 feet square off the living room with access to the rear garden. There was a small pantry under the stairs and a store cupboard in the front bedroom. That was it! The 'parlour' or guest room opened out directly onto the street.

Mom and Dad had the back bedroom while myself, my brother Philip and later my sister Sally shared the front bedroom. I remember the bedroom had wall mounted gas outlets with taps where gas lights had been. They were still connected and could be turned on although at some time I recall them being removed and sealed. The store cupboard in the front bedroom was large with access to the roof space. In it was a box containing wartime gas masks and other items. The cupboard always seemed scary to a young child's imagination!

Furnishings and décor were basic – yellow distemper on the wall (suppose similar to today's emulsion), lino on the floors (no carpets). There was an old folding table, sideboard, wooden chairs and an arm chair. The parlour had an old settee and an armchair. A tall kitchen cabinet was kept in the living room as there was not room in the kitchen! On top of the kitchen cabinet was an old valve radio. The bedrooms had two old wardrobes and a chest of drawers, good job we didn't have many clothes!

My father worked in a rolling mill in Saltley and then as a 'commissionaire' at the Metro-Cammell works in Washwood Heath. He had a uniform in which he took great pride. He later progressed (I think it was progress) to be an electrician's mate at Morris Commercial Cars in Adderley Park. He was able to assist me in securing an apprenticeship at MCC in 1960. My mother had stopped working to raise the family and only returned to work in the 1970s.

Life was basic and frugal but I never recall going hungry. There were few luxuries, a week's holiday in a caravan in Rhyl, days out to the Lickey Hills, Cannon Hill Park or Chelmsley Wood. All by train, tram or bus, my parents never owned a car.

There was also visiting and being visited by relatives. My mother was one of ten children, my father one of four. They lived in Kingstanding, Billesley, Yardley Wood, Lea Village, Highgate and Short Heath. Family ties were strong and regular contact was made.

Aunt Mary lived in Highgate in a back to back house close to the centre of Birmingham. I remember visiting and walking from her house to the Bull Ring markets. On the way we passed through the wholesale market area. I recall sheep and pigs being herded along the street on the way to the slaughterhouse, bleating and squealing with the occasional breakaway being pursued by the market traders! The streets were cobbled and slippery with animal excreta, spilt fruit and veg and water.

Aunt Margaret lived in a council house in Lea Village – luxury! Bathroom, inside toilet, large garden. Her husband had died young leaving her to raise four daughters by herself. It was not far to walk from there to Marston Green and Chelmsley Wood, it was all open country then and many happy times were had.

I only knew one set of grandparents, my mom's parents. They lived in Yardley Wood in a fairly modern council house. My gran always wore a long full dress with a flowery pinafore over it. Her hair was always scraped back into a bun. My grandad was a large man never without his pipe and flat cap. There was always a 'stew' on the go served with a chunk of bread. The highlight of a visit was when she opened the toy cupboard. There was a multi coloured spinning top which hummed as it turned, a monkey which climbed a ladder and a spiral rod with a coloured wheel which went up and down the spiral as it was turned over. Simple, but it kept us amused for hours!

My Gran died a few years before my grandad. After she died he would come to our house most Sundays. He would arrive mid morning and have his feet washed and toenails trimmed. I was sent to the outdoor for two bottles of 'Nut Brown' ale which he would have with his lunch. We would then walk him back to the bus stop mid afternoon. To me it was a pleasant few hours, I enjoyed his stories, the smell of his pipe but heaven knows what my father thought of this encroachment onto his Sunday!

One of my earliest memories of living in Alum Rock is looking out of the back bedroom window at deep snow. A neighbour was digging a path to his garden gate, I could just see his head above the snow! This must have been the terrible winter of 1947.

So my formative years from 1946 until 1965 were spent in this modest home with parents who in spite of hardships did their level best to give their children a decent upbringing.

Most of my childhood memories are happy ones. Mendip Avenue was a cul-de-sac which made it fairly safe to play in though there was little traffic anyway. At the end of the Avenue were two brick air raid shelters each containing several rooms. They had been bricked up but a way in was soon found! They were great 'dens' even if a little scary and they could be a fort, castle anything that the imagination wanted them to be.

Beyond the shelters was a large area of open ground known locally as the 'tip'. This was our adventure playground, our Alton Towers our Disneyland. The origins of the tip are unclear but it had a range of 'features'. There was a sandy area, areas of rough long grass and weeds, several small hillocks and a patch of land containing a range of small coloured glass tubes and particles.

Nowadays I imagine it would be declared a health and safety risk and fenced off, however no one ever seemed to come to any harm. The tip was the 'Wild West' with cowboys and indians, Sherwood Forest, a strange forbidden planet, a wartime battlefield, Camelot with King Arthur and his Knights.

Our imagination was triggered by radio programmes 'Journey into Space', 'Dick Barton' and the numerous comics read. I remember the Dandy, Beano, Eagle, Topper, Beazer, Film Fun and several feature comics. These would be swapped with mates on a regular basis. I could be a cowboy (Lash Larue, Wyatt Earp, Hopalong Cassidy, Roy Rogers or Gene Autrey) or an indian, usually Geronimo. I could be Robin Hood, Sheriff of Nottingham, Sir Lancelot, Dan Dare, Dick Turpin, Biggles or Superman saving the world. A group of us would spend hours acting out scenes, finding old clothes, cardboard boxes, anything to make costumes and props. We would also build 'dens' using planks, corrugated iron, old wash tubs, old mats and linoleum.

There were problems, children from neighbouring streets who were not part of our 'gang' would attempt to disrupt our games, destroy our 'dens', pick fights, throw stones. No change there then! Local rivalry, tribal warfare, power struggles have always been part of life.

The 'tip' was also our Wembley stadium our Oval for football and cricket although the pitch was not quite up to the same standard! In later years it became a courting ground, a place for meeting girls, a kiss, a fumble, nothing more, all very innocent!

Imagination was also fired by visits to the local cinema. My local was the Grand, a contradiction in terms if ever there was one. It was situated on the Alum Rock Rd a few minutes walk from home and is still there used as a carpet warehouse. Every Saturday morning there was a children's club and we would all queue up under a covered shelter alongside the cinema waiting for the doors to open at 10.00. A uniformed doorman tried to keep order, but with several hundred excited youngsters he had no chance!

Once in there would be a variety of short films and cartoons followed by the main feature usually a Western followed by a serial – my memory is of Flash Gordon with Buster Crabbe. Throughout the performance there would be cheers for the heroes, boos for the villains, lots of throwing of sweet wrappers and other missiles. The projector would sometimes break down or the film break accompanied by jeers and foot stamping.

I recall going to the Grand one Saturday afternoon on my own to see Ali Baba and the Forty Thieves. A few minutes into the film there appeared on screen an evil looking arab wielding a long curving knife. I shot out of the cinema scared stiff and ran home, I told my mother I had lost my money and couldn't get in! In the same area was the posher Rock cinema, the Capitol and the mock Tudor Beaufort.

This was the early 1950s, no television only a radio for entertainment. Programmes like Workers Playtime, The Goon Show, Educating Archie, Round the Horne, Down Your Way and on Sunday Family Favourites request show. Music was big bands like Ted Heath, Joe Loss, Mantovani and singers Dickie Valentine, Rosemary Clooney, Bing, Vic Damone and a young Shirley Bassey. When Rock "Roll and pop music came on the scene in the late 50" I used to tune into Radio Luxembourg, very faint and erratic, to hear the latest music. Needless to say my parents thought it was an awful row, Elvis was a bad influence, it will soon pass!

I was in my third year at Saltley Grammar school when the pop revolution started. I remember the Capitol cinema near to the school showing the film 'Blackboard Jungle' with Bill Haley and Rock around the Clock. Pupils gathered outside the cinema at lunchtimes to look at the photos and practise the new dance craze. Unfortunately the film created a storm when cinemagoers went into an excited frenzy and ripped out seats. Soon afterwards came the hip shaking Elvis 'the Pelvis' Presley with Heartbreak Hotel, All Shook Up and Don't be Cruel.

What exciting days they were, parents horrified as their children were transformed, wanting record players, records, new style clothes, flared skirts, bobby socks, different hairstyles, burgers, chewing gum. Then it was British Pop with Cliff, the Beatles, Rolling Stones, Mersey sound, Brum sound, everyone wanting a guitar, wanting to form a band and become a star.

Neighbours were important, they would help each other out, be eyes and ears, providing gossip and entertainment. In Mendip Avenue and the adjoining Tarry Rd, Nansen Rd and Gowan Rd I had lots of friends. We would play in each others houses and parents would get to know each other. Word soon get round if there was a problem or someone needed help. Neighbours would get together for special occasions and events, there were always plenty of willing hands.

I remember Bonfire Nights, collecting rubbish for the bonfire, making a Guy 'spare a penny mister', the day itself, patiently waiting for the dark. The bonfire was built on the 'tip' lit up, potatoes and chestnuts roasting, beer and pop, singing and fireworks carefully lit by parents – light the blue touch paper and retire to a safe distance! Of course it wasn't all like that, we would buy fireworks especially bangers and jumping jacks and use them in various ways. My favourite was to put a banger Mighty Atom under an old tin can and watch it hurtle into the air. A banger put into an unsuspecting householders dustbin would explode with a loud 'whoomp' bringing them running out.

Christmas was really special, the anticipation would start in December not in August like nowadays. Decorations, home made streamers and a tree would go up a few days before Christmas. There would be a visit to see Father Christmas arrive with Uncle Holly at Lewis's store in Old Square city centre. A group of us would go carol singing to raise some money to buy presents, we had no fears about going round the streets in the evening.

Christmas Eve was so exciting, there would be some extra special food on the table, pork pie, pickles, ham, cheese, mince pies. Neighbours would pop in bringing a card and maybe a gift or we would go to their house. It was off to bed early leaving a carrot and a glass of sherry by the fireplace for Santa and Rudolph. A pillow case would be left at the end of the bed then it was sleep, no peeping! Early morning wake up to find the pillowcase now contained a few presents, an orange, apple and a walnut. One of the presents was always a book, Rupert was usual or one of the annuals Beano, Dandy or Eagle. I loved, and still do, the Rupert books with their pictures and stories of his adventures.

Christmas lunch was a great treat – chicken, sage and onion stuffing, sprouts and home made xmas pudding. The pudding was steamed in a muslin cloth for hours and always contained a threepenny bit or a silver sixpence.

Christmas entertainment was also home made, no TV, no transport, no shops open, no pubs open. There were games, music off the radio, storytelling and of course the new toys to play with. Neighbours would pop in for a drink late afternoon or evening or we would go to theirs taking our toys to show friends.

New Year's Evening was also special, the radio would be on, tables and chairs pushed back to make a small dance floor and we would jig around, my mom trying to teach me dance steps. At midnight we would go outside through the back door pick a piece of coal up from the coalhouse and go in through the front door – old year out, new year in, coal to bring luck! Factory hooters would be sounded and church bells rung, neighbours would wish each other well and everyone then retired to bed ready for work the next day (New Year's Day was not a holiday then).

As mentioned previously, the only form of heating was coal fires and the coalman would deliver sacks of coal on a regular basis. He had a small lorry on which were the sacks of coal and a pair of scales. He wore overalls and a leather apron with an extension over his shoulders and head for protection when carrying the sacks on his back. He was always as black as the coal he was carrying! The coal was supplied in an assortment of different size lumps. I often had the job of breaking the lumps up with a hammer into smaller usable pieces. The coal was supplemented by any wood or logs we could find locally. I also recall going to the gasworks and queuing for a bag of coke. This was a by-product of gasmaking and it gave off a fierce heat when burned and produced less ash.

There were three problems with coal fires, firstly lighting it, secondly clearing away the ashes and thirdly having the chimney swept. Lighting was simply paper, wood and matches except it was often slow to get going. This is where the 'draw tin' came into use. This was a flat piece of metal the size of the grate aperture with a handle attached. It would be placed against the grate with just a small gap at the bottom. This had the effect of causing air to rush in and fan the fire into action. Sometimes the drawtin would be glowing red hot! My father would increase the efficiency of the drawtin by putting a sheet of newspaper over it to seal the gaps around the edges. Occasionally the newspaper would burst into flames causing a short panic while it was put out! Clearing away the ashes was a daily messy job, the ashes were either put into the dustbin or spread on the garden. The fire would sometimes not burn very well and smoke would come into the room, there would also be small falls of soot from the chimney onto the fire. Time to call in the chimney sweep.

The chimney sweep would arrive with a collection of poles and brushes and several covers to put over furniture and the grate. A circular brush would be attached to a short pole which was put through a hole in the cover. Longer poles would then be attached and the brush pushed up the chimney with pushing, pulling, twisting and turning. Showers of soot would descend down the chimney most of it trapped behind the cover but inevitably some escaping into the room. We would rush outside and cheer as the brush appeared at the chimney top. If a chimney was not swept then the soot would sometimes catch fire and there would be a sheet of flame coming out of the chimney pot! Some people deliberately set the chimney on fire to avoid paying to have it swept. It was dangerous and could result in a house fire or a cracked chimney or pot, apart from the sooty fall out into neighbours gardens! I remember when a gas fire was installed in the parlour room, bliss!

Food was fairly basic but I never remember going hungry. There were lots of 'stews' with pork ribs or breast of lamb, loads of veg and a chunk of bread to mop up the gravy – delicious! There were other things like brawn, tripe, chitterlings and chawl – all offal or cheaper cuts of meat. Rabbit was often used in a stew, I remember them hanging in the butchers or at the market and my mother skinning them.

Saturdays my mother would nearly always go into 'town' to the market and return with fish and shellfish. Kippers or smoked haddock, whelks or mussels boiled in a pan the smell permeating the house.

Sundays there might be a pork chop, a piece of boiled bacon or hock, I never remember a 'roast' joint. Puddings as they are today were non existent but home made rice pudding with a skin on the top and nutmeg was a favourite. Another was jelly and blancmange with a slice of bread and marg.

Other regular meals were bread and jam, boiled eggs, bread and lard, beans on toast and sausage and mash. I do recall breakfast was nearly always Scotts porridge oats, the packet had a picture of a kilted strongman (you will look like this if you eat your porridge!).

Drink was mainly tea, Typhoo of course, made in Birmingham! Coffee was the treacly looking Camp essence in a bottle, strong tasting. I drank a lot of milk and water, often a pint in one go.

The milkman and baker delivered daily in their horse drawn carts. I loved and at the same time was scared of the horses, they seemed so big. They had nosebags containing what looked like Scotts porridge oats, this was supplemented by titbits put in by customers. If a horse 'pooped' in the street I would get a shovel and bucket and collect it to go on the garden or allotment for manure.

My father had an allotment in Limetree Rd about half a mile away. The family would help out with digging, planting, weeding and watering, and of course harvesting! There was a shed on the plot with table and chairs, a real home from home.

There was not much money coming into the household. My father was not well paid, my mother was not working with three children to look after. I remember my mother buying items for the home from a company called Sloans, paying back weekly. A man called to collect the payments and try to persuade my mother to buy more. Sometimes we couldn't afford to pay and would hide in the pantry when he called, pretending to be out.

Generally speaking life was basic but reasonably happy. As a child I always seemed to have something to do, playing out with friends, reading, radio, drawing, jobs in the house or out visiting relatives.

I had quite a strict upbringing, no matter what hardships were endured we had to be clean and well turned out. Washed (don't forget behind the ears), hair combed, shoes cleaned, shirt tucked in. The house was kept clean and tidy, everything had its place. Meals had to be eaten unless ill, like it or not, nothing was wasted, any leftovers were turned into another meal – bubble and squeak!

Courtesy and politeness were expected, swearing was absolutely taboo – I remember getting a cuff round the ear for using the word 'bloody'. A slap on the legs or a stick across the buttocks, often the broomhandle, was given for misdemeanours! Short, sharp and very effective.

Some specific memories stick in my mind:

When there was a thunderstorm, and they often seemed very severe, we would 'hide' in the pantry. On one occasion my father had made some ginger beer using a kit which was all the rage at the time and stored the bottles in the pantry. The heat and humidity of the storm caused the corks to pop out of the bottles and we had a shower in ginger beer!

Monday was washday, all the dirty clothes accumulated during the week were put into the wash tub. This was a metal circular container with corrugations down the sides. It would be half filled with hot water heated in pans and buckets on the gas cooker, Persil soap flakes were added along with the mysterious 'blue bag'. I now know that this was a chemical whitener. A wooden 'dolly' was used to mash the washing with a twisting, turning and lifting motion. When finished the washing was rinsed with cold water and put through the mangle, a device with a handle and two rollers for squeezing the water out of the washing. Finally the clothes were pegged out on the washing line or hung onto a clothes horse in front of the fire. My mother eventually obtained a second hand twin tub in the late 1960s and a Hotpoint washing machine in the 1980s!

Clothes were fit for purpose, fashion and designer clothes were unheard of or seen only in films. Up to age 11 I wore short trousers held up by braces, plain shirts, pullovers, grey socks and black shoes. In winter there was a heavy top coat, scarf and balaclava. No anoraks, sports wear, hoods, trainers, baseball caps or sweatshirts. I had new long trousers for grammar school, a blazer, cap, scarf and gaberdine raincoat, my parents must have skimped to afford those. In my later teens I eventually caught up with fashion, bought myself winklepicker pointed shoes, a 'bumfreezer' jacket and coloured shirts! I can remember the girls in flared dresses, bouffant hairstyles, stockings and suspenders!

Parents retained the utilitarian clothes although I remember my mom treating herself to a 'mock' fur coat, she was so proud of it!

Shopping was mainly local. There were five corner shops within 5/10 minutes walk each selling a mixture of groceries, bread, sweets, newspapers, cigarettes. Each had its regular customers often allowing them to buy items and put it 'on the slate' to be paid at the end of the week.

Alum Rock Rd was the major shopping area with grocers Jesters, Wrensons, Maypole and Co-op. Greengrocers were Ted Haynes, Browns and the Co-op. Butchers were Latchfords, Smarts, Bywaters and City. There was a Woolworths, Lucas Hardware, Kiddiland for toys, The Shop That Stands on a Bob (bargain store). Freeman Hardy Willis, Bates, Fosters and the good old Co-op sold clothes and footwear. Braggs bakery was always popular, the smell of baking attracting people, as did the smell from the Highfield fish and chip shop. A pawnshop with the three balls hanging outside and a money lender did good trade.

Today Alum Rock Rd is still a vibrant shopping centre with a similar range of shops but mainly Asian owned and catering for the Asian community, Halal butcher, Sari shop, spices and naan bread. Parents of a school friend of mine, Leslie Nutt, had a sewing machine shop near the old Rock Cinema. It is still there, same owners, perhaps indicative of the Asian passion for dressmaking.

Schooldays bring memories. Junior school I clearly recall country dancing lessons, holding hands with girls Yuk! Also on Friday afternoons there were no lessons, we were treated to watching Charlie Chaplin and Laurel and Hardy films. The school playground at Nansen Rd school sloped steeply, great in the winter in icy weather for sliding down! Not much memory of the actual lessons but I must have learned something as I passed my eleven plus for a place at Saltley Grammar School.

What a change! Moving round to different classrooms, four or five different teachers in one day, teachers wearing gowns and in a couple of cases mortar boards! Strict discipline, the cane or slipper across hand or backside for talking or eating in class, lateness, not doing homework, not in uniform. As nowadays teachers varied in their discipline, popularity and effectiveness. I recall a history teacher whose lessons consisted of copying pages out of a text book or from Banda copies while she sat and read a book!

One teacher had a habit of putting his foot up on the front desk in the class while he talked. He wore trousers with turnups and the pupil at the said desk, encouraged by the class would put pennies and halfpennies into the turnups. He never seemed to notice and went off to his next class where they would be added to by another pupil and so on. They would be removed and returned later in the day, the idea being to see how many could be put in, I never knew the final result!

My parents, rest in peace, took me on holiday the first two weeks in September 1955 when I was due to start at grammar school. Imagine starting two weeks after everyone else, new systems, no friends, strange lessons. On the first day I remember algebra $x + y = 2x$, what is this mixing numbers and letters together? I went home baffled and in tears. Next day there was chemistry with bunsen burners, test tubes and coloured chemicals. I was much happier!

I was caned once and slippered once. The cane was for wearing bright fluorescent orange socks, strictly against rules but the fashion of the time.

The author aged 15 in the back garden of Mendip Avenue. The houses in the background were superior, they had a bathroom!

The slipper was for when the teacher went out of the room and the class started banging their feet on the wooden floor including me, I was nearest the door when he came back and was made an example of!

It took some time to adjust to grammar school and the first year I was slow to, learn, however once I got going I did well and finished up taking my GCE 'O' levels in four years instead of five. There is more about the implications of this elsewhere in this book.

As a grammar school pupil I had to take a lot of stick from other youngsters and some adults. Name calling 'grammar grub', 'swot' 'posh' were common, this was often accompanied by my cap being thrown over a hedge or the contents of my satchel being emptied out. However I enjoyed my time at grammar school and the education gave me an excellent grounding for the life ahead. The discipline, respect, courtesy expected and received is sadly lacking in much of today's society.

When I reached 21 years of age I had a party at the house in Mendip Avenue. My mother put on a buffet and my mates bought in all the booze. There were lots of 'party 7's' (7 pint casks of beer), bottles of beer and spirits. It was an all male party, none of us were dating girls regularly, so it was eating, drinking, music and rugby songs. The following day it was like a warzone, bodies everywhere, food and drink unfinished. It was a good 'do' some my mates still remember.

In 1962 my brother Philip died at the age of 14 after many years of illness. This had a dramatic effect on the family especially my mother. Ironically, after years of trying to get a better house especially with my brother being ill, we moved to a new council house on the Castle Vale estate, the old Castle Bromwich airfield. At last – inside toilet, bathroom, hot water on tap, central heating, reasonable garden, even car parking space! My mother was rejuvenated by this move and went back to work part time which helped in getting over the loss of Philip.

I moved from Castle Vale in 1968 when I got married but have worked on the estate as a community worker since 1993 seeing the regeneration process taking place. That's another story.

Chapter 3

EARLY YEARS – THE LOCAL SCENE

I was now probably 9 or 10 years old. In the years 1952/53, railways were still the main means of transporting people and freight. I was living in a two up two down Victorian terraced house in a cul-de-sac in Alum Rock. No bathroom, outside toilet, no hot water, only a coal fire for heating and it seemed wonderful! Saucepans of water heated on the ancient gas cooker every Sunday evening ready for the weekly bath in the oval tub – me, my brother and sister in quick succession! Adjacent to the house was a 'bomb site' where buildings had been destroyed in the war. The cul-de-sac and the bomb site or 'tip' as we called it were our playground. There was little traffic and games were safely played in the street (or 'orse road as we called it). Chase games, daring games, hopscotch, jackstones and marbles (marlies) all had their seasons together with the ever popular ball games.There was little to disturb these games – the occasional car or lorry, the horse drawn milk and bakers carts, the 'rag and bone' man with his call of 'rag bone, old iron'. A quick dash indoors to find some unwanted item and an exchange was made for a goldfish or a live fluffy chick. In spite of careful tending these 'pets' never seemed to survive long and joy turned to tears.

Alum Rock was, and still is, a densely populated district approximately 4 miles from the centre of the city. Heavy industry in the shape of car factories (Morris and Wolsley), rolling mills, carriage and wagon works and a myriad small firms dominated the area and provided local employment. Dominating the scene and filling the area with smoke and smell was the gasworks at Saltley and Nechells. In the mornings the factory whistles or 'bulls' as they were known, each with its own distinct sound, chivvied workers along to their workplaces.

In the background was the constant sound of railways – steam engines, the clatter of shunting, the clickety-clack of passenger trains. I would lie in bed and, particularly on clear winter nights, listen to the workings of the local railways. The sights, sounds and smells associated with this era are easily bought to mind – smoke from domestic coal fires, factory noise and fumes, 'pig bins', horse droppings, gasworks and the sweeter smell of bread baking at Braggs! Rows of terraced houses, neighbours 'canting' or 'gabbing', the corner shops 'open all hours', the 'Grand' cinema and its posher neighbour the 'Rock'.

Local youngsters soon formed into 'gangs' usually associated with an area or common interest. I quickly found friends with an interest in trainspotting. This was helped by my class teacher at Nansen Road school, Mr Hesketh who was a railway enthusiast. Nansen Road school had a view towards Ward End Park through which passed the Aston-Stechford railway line. Trains were infrequent, just as well as every time a train passed Mr Hesketh would take binoculars out of his desk 'spot' the number and write it on the blackboard!

If trains had been more frequent heaven knows what would have happened to my education! Mr Hesketh took the whole class out on day trips to spotting venues, more of this later.

So the bug had bitten and with notebook and pencil I started spotting in the local area. The map (page 38) shows the most popular sites and I will endeavour to recall memories and incidents from these.

1. LUDLOW ROAD BRIDGE

This was the 'smashing place' my friends had told me about and which had stimulated my imagination. It was in fact a narrow bridge across the Birmingham-London line near to Adderley Park Station. Road traffic was banned across the bridge, making it a safe haven for spotting. The line was very busy with London trains, Coventry and Rugby locals, freight trains and occasional trains to Peterborough and East Anglia.

The London trains were usually headed by Jubilees with the odd 'black five', Royal Scot or Patriot. Common ones were – 45647 Sturdee, 45688 Polyphemus, 45733 Novelty, 45734 Meteor, 45737 Atlas, 45738 Samson, 45740 Munster, 45741 Leinster, 45742 Connaught, 45703 Thunderer, 45514 Holyhead, 45523 Bangor, 45545 Planet, 46128 The Lovatt Scouts, 46154 The Hussar, 46170 British Legion and of course 46129 The Scottish Horse.

Local trains were entrusted to 2-6-4 tanks with black fives on the semi-fasts. Compounds were still in evidence and were sometimes coupled to a London train with a Jubilee – a spectacular sight! (40933, 40936, 41162 and 41168 were noted) There was a through train from Norwich which generally was hauled by a black five but occasionally sported an ER B1 a rare sight. Freight trains were always interesting with Hughes and Stanier "crabs", Ivatt moguls, Fowler 4F's, black fives, stanier 8F's and my own favourites ex LNWR 0-8-0 (duck 8's and super D's). An additional bonus to Ludlow Rd Bridge was the adjoining allotments – spotters never went hungry although they often had stomach ache!

2. WARD END PARK

Ward End park was and still is a large green oasis in a heavily built up and industrialised area. It was 10 minutes walk from my home in Alum Rock and as a child was a wonderful place to play in. It had a large boating and fishing pool, cricket field, bowling green, tennis courts, hothouse, cafeteria and a large playground. I remember in the summer months a large marquee was erected by the council and variety shows were put on including talent contests for up and coming pop groups.

It was also a favourite venue for meeting members of the opposite sex. I remember coyly 'chatting up' a young lady and was just starting to get to know her better when she announced she was moving to Bournemouth! My first love ended in a broken heart, I think I was probably 14/15 years of age!

In addition to all these features and events in the park, right through the middle ran a railway line! This was a Sundays only "spotting" venue as it was the New Street avoiding line and only carried appreciable traffic when the main line between Rugby and Stafford was in possession of the engineers, always on Sundays. The first train was always the "Carlisle freight" and this usually provided the most interesting motive power – often a black five or Jubilee from Carlisle MPD returning Northwards. There followed a succession of Liverpool, Manchester, Blackpool and North Wales expresses before the Royal Scot with impressive headboard, coach indicator boards and tailboard. This was always a spotless Princess Royal or Coronation Pacific locomotive.

Hoards of spotters gathered in Ward End Park, for many it was the only chance to see Pacific locomotives and the famous titled trains. There was only one signal in view, a down distant and the approach of trains was heralded by the keenest eyed yelling "smoke sighted!" Sometimes the diversions carried on into late evening and a keen hoard of spotters would wait equipped with torches for the last train.

Unfortunately, as always, there was a gang who were derisive of "train spotting" and made frequent raids hurling sticks and stones and generally bullying with the intention of disrupting the enthusiasts. Nevertheless the spotting continued and the bullies were gradually subdued, especially when Transport police caught them placing bricks onto the line!

I have a record of a day at Ward End Park on Sunday 18th September 1960. The following locomotives were recorded; 45291, (Up freight), 45380 (Up passenger), D5 (Up Ulster Express), 45666 (Down freight), D289 (Down Royal Scot), 46136 (Up express), 45235, 46110 (double headed down Merseyside Express), 46208 (Down Express), D222 (down express), 45734 (up express), 45584 (down express), 46204 (up express), D220 (up express), 46111 (up express), 46161 (up express), 45726 (down freight), 46127 (up express), D231 (up express), D235 (down express), D234 (down express), D214 (up express), 71000 (down express). A total of 15 steam engines and 8 diesels.

Nine months later on Sunday 26th June 1961 the following were recorded: D302, D319, 45603, D337, D331, D221, D298, 45598, 46129, D342, 70042, D309, D213, D288, D289, 46229, D310, 46250, D291, 45624, D333. A total of 14 diesel and 7 steam locomotives – a reversal of nine months earlier!

An unusual combination, Class 40 diesel D297 and BR standard class five 73033 at Ward End Park on Sunday 6th November 1960 with a down express.

3. ASTON CHURCH ROAD

This was a boy's delight, especially if he was a train spotter. Here there was a large expanse of waste ground, alongside the Birmingham-Derby line at the point where the Birmingham avoiding line crossed it on a high viaduct. There was also a maze of sidings and a spur for Camphill banking engines and a branch into the Metro-Cammell carriage and wagon works. If one became bored with spotting then there were several streams and culverts to explore and fall into! The whole scene was overshadowed by enormous gasholders and the air was filled with the pungent smell of the local gasworks!

One feature of this site was a sleeper crossing over the sidings and freight lines to a cabin which was presumably a yard controller's office and crew signing on point. This provided a means of getting really close to the trains, in fact looking back it was lucky that no-one was injured. However, this closeness enabled spotters to become friendly with many railway men and footplate rides and guards van rides were frequent! If one was really lucky, and I was, only once, then a footplate ride on a Camp Hill banker could be had. This was a round trip of approximately 6 miles to the Camp Hill summit and back. There was a condition on these rides that as the engine passed Saltley station and MPD the "Stowaway" should duck out of sight in case the "gaffer" should be on the lookout!

As always, some of the reckless spotters spoilt the scene by climbing aboard slow moving wagons, using the brake bar as a step-up. It was not long before railway police began to patrol the area and several prosecutions were made. It was several weeks before spotters were brave enough to venture back to Aston Church Road.

As previously mentioned this was the Birmingham to Derby mainline with Northeast to Southwest expresses, locals to Derby and Leicester and freight to all parts of the country.

The expresses were headed by Jubilees from Bristol, Sheffield, Leeds, Derby and Leicester. 45572 Eire, 45576 Bombay, 45577 Bengal, 45585 Hyderabad, 45590 Travancore, 45594 Bhopal, 45607 Fiji, 45610 Gold Coast (later Ghana), 45626 Seychelles, 45651 Shovell, 45654 Hood, 45656 Cochrane, 45660 Rooke, 45662 Kempenfelt, 45663 Jarvis, 45664 Nelson, 45682 Trafalgar, 45690 Leander, 45699 Galatea, 45725 Repulse were frequently "spotted".

Double-heading was common, especially on summer Saturdays, when the Jubilee was piloted by a compound, a Stanier black five or a standard class 5. There was one challenger to the Jubilee's monopoly in the form of patriot 45509 "The Derbyshire Yeomany" which often worked Derby-Bristol trains. She was affectionately known as the "Derby Yo-Yo" and always made an impressive if somewhat ungainly sight with the parallel "blinkers" (smoke deflectors) and narrow tender.

Local trains were worked by a vast variety of engines including Stanier black fives, Ivatt Moguls (flying pigs), Fowler 4F's, (Duck 6's), 2-6-4 tanks, Johnson 4-4-0 2P's and compounds, Fowler Moguls (crabs) and standard class 5's.

The passenger trains were mainly worked by engines from Saltley, Derby, Bristol Barrow Road, Sheffield Mill houses, Gloucester, Leicester and Nottingham. After a few months "spotting" it was possible to collect almost every mainline loco from these depots and "cops" on passenger trains became rare.

Summer Saturdays were the exception when locos from Leeds (Holbeck and Farnley Junction), York, Bradford and other unusual areas would appear. There was also the occasional rarity, an Eastern Region B1 or V2.

Freight provided the greatest interest with a wide range of engines from all over the country. Washwood Heath sidings, Camphill Bank, the gasworks sidings and the Metro-Cammell spur all led to an array of interesting movements.

Engines working to and from the marshalling yards at Washwood Heath or Water Orton from Saltley MPD would travel in 3's, 4's, 5's and even 6's coupled together. There would always be 2 or 3 Johnson 2F or 3F 0-6-0's in the banking spur and there was always a freight waiting to be banked and another waiting behind it. The 0-6-0 diesel "growlers" were backwards and forwards constantly shunting the wagons. The gasworks private owner locos fussed about in the background. Bliss!

It was frustrating at times when all the signals were off and everything arrived at the same time! More so if the Growler had just pulled some wagons in front of you in the line of sight!

A typical array of freight locos spotted on one morning was – 43645, 48217, 73144, 75022, 49210, 44388, 47424, 43822, 42854, 92127, 92120, 12039, 43468, 90723, 48492, 48682, 48650, 44278, 44560, 47994, (Garratt), 92025 (Crosti), 43284, 44666, 58261, D3168 PLUS the following on passenger makes for an interesting morning: 61195, 73019, 45682, 43047, 45610 (no nameplate) 45648, 41121, 40700, 75004.

The spur to Metro-Cammell produced some eye opening items – stock for countries which we had never heard of. They were towed out by a growler and then attached behind a loco for the first part of their long journey. London underground stock was also a regular sight and we even started collecting the numbers!

The 'High Level' line which, as the map shows was the same line as the Ward End Park venue was only used occasionally. Motive power consisted of Aston and Bescot 'crabs', moguls, 0-8-0's and 8F's. Aston Church Road was a popular place but could be dangerous and was frequented by police who took the view that all train spotters were up to no good.

4. SALTLEY STATION

Saltley station site is now only recognisable by the bricked up entrance at the apex of Saltley viaduct and the wide gap between the up and down fast lines where the island platform stood. Access was from the viaduct carrying the A47 road over the River Rea, Fazeley Canal, Birmingham-Derby mainline, gasworks lines and the coke work sidings. A wide, totally enclosed wooden staircase led down to the island platform.

Footsteps on the stairs were greatly amplified by this 'tunnel', a factor which was useful to station staff but not to train spotters trying to sneak onto the platform.

Some station staff actively discouraged train spotters, some did not mind so long as they were not in the way and one utilised the extra hands for portering and cleaning. It did not take long to work out the' shift' system and to know when and when not to go to Saltley.

Although the same locos were spotted here as at Aston Church Road and the two were less than a mile apart, the range of sights and sounds were totally different. The gas and coke works adjoined the station and it was fascinating watching the maze of hissing pipes, valves, smoking stacks, rattling conveyers and cascading coke. Add to this the noisy shunting of wagons and the fairly frequent loading of barges on the canal, the overhead crane moving stock piles of coke and the roar of the River Rea down its culvert. Little wonder passengers did not linger! The whole scene was overpowered by the acrid stench of the gasworks.

My fondest memory of Saltley station is standing on the platform at dusk and watching the twin lights of an express approaching bound for Birmingham. The curve through the station caused the locos to lurch and sway, almost hitting the platform edge. The noise level built up to a crescendo culminating in the blast from the chimney deflecting from the viaduct, leaving behind a cloud of smoke, soot and steam through which glimpses of passengers in the dimly lit carriages could be seen.

Saltley was the ticket collecting station for local trains into Birmingham and trains were held here while station staff went through the train, New Street being an open station. One dodge was to wait until the ticket inspector had gone through the first coach and then jump on for a free ride into New Street. The problem was, getting back. It either meant walking, paying the fare to get back or 'dodging' again. 'Dodging' the return trip either meant being in the last coach for a quick get out up the stairs at Saltley or the first coach when one could alight and stand on the platform, book and pencil in hand, as though you had been there all the time. It was unlucky if you were spotted as Saltley was a busy station, with lots of railway workers alighting to walk to the shed.

There was a signal box at the east end of the platform, and if the right 'bobby' was on duty, a warm seat and a cup of tea could be had, usually in return for carrying a few bucketfuls of coal up to the box. There were six tracks running through Saltley station, three each side of the platform. There were times when every track had one or more trains on it, it was a train spotter's dream.

Stanier Black '5' 44941 rushes a parcels train through Saltley station, 12th June 1962. Gasworks and sidings in background B Dunckley.

5. LANDOR STREET AND BRICKYARD CROSSING

Landor Street passes beneath the Birmingham Camphill avoiding line and the Birmingham-Derby line. It also runs parallel to the Birmingham-London line. The lines forming a triangle in which there used to be some waste ground, ideal for viewing all three lines. The big problem here was that it was so busy, trains would be on all three lines, sometimes in both directions and you needed three pairs of eyes!

Spotting here combined the Saltley and Ludlow road venues. The only locos missed were those going 'on shed' from Bromford and Washwood Heath. It was also possible, depending on the 'bobby' in the signal box, to climb steps to a point alongside the Birmingham-London line where the triangle could be seen and also the loop from the London line to the Camphill avoiding line. This was not used very often, certainly not like it is used today.

Brickyard crossing was outside the triangle, on the Camphill line. It was popular, partly because it was exciting to climb on the crossing gate whilst an 8F pounded up the bank, ably supported by one or more 3F 0-6-0's in the rear. The main attraction though was that the box was nearly always open to visitors. To stand in the box, occasionally attempt to 'pull off' a signal and on rare occasions open the crossing gates was a schoolboy's dream.

'Duck 6' Fowler 0-6-0 4F 44123 makes a vigorous attack on Camp Hill bank at Brickyard Crossing on 15th October 1960. The photo was taken from the signal box steps.

6. HALL ROAD

Hall Road runs parallel to the line from New Street to Sutton and Walsall near to Vauxhall and Duddeston station. The line was mainly used by local trains and with very little freight traffic, it was not a good place for spotting – with one exception.

Crewe works used the Glasgow-Birmingham train as a running – in turn for ex-works locos. It arrived at Vauxhall-Duddeston station at 5.30pm and left its coaches in the hands of a shunter for stabling and ran light engine to Aston shed. This could produce anything from a Crewe "Royal Scot" to a Scottish "Clan". Examples of locos seen on this train are: "46112 Sherwood Forester", "71000 Duke of Gloucester", and "70054 Dornoch Firth". The loco would also work an earlier train arriving approximately midday. Word would soon get round if it was an unusual or rare loco and a crowd of spotters would descend on Hall Road.

Adjacent to Hall Road were rows of Victorian terraced houses, many empty and awaiting demolitions. This was a playground for us while waiting for the "Glasgow". We took it upon ourselves to help demolishing the houses and would push over some of the obviously dilapidated walls. I remember once we decided to save the demolition men some time and push down a wall which looked as though it would fall down by itself at any time. We heaved and pushed and eventually a large piece of wall fell. Imagine our surprise when a man came running out of the adjacent house brandishing a stick, we had just demolished his outside toilet! We missed the Glasgow that day and it was only when passing by on a bus and noticing all the houses had been demolished a couple of weeks later that we resumed our visits to Hall Road.

7. NEW STREET STATION

Surprisingly my visits to New Street were not frequent, probably because once the locos on passenger duty had been 'spotted' it was only rarely that a strange loco was to be seen. The freight trains provided the widest variety of motive power and freight trains by passed New Street, using the Camp Hill line.

However, New Street did have its attractions. The station was split down the middle by Queens Drive, platforms 1-6 were the 'LNWR' side and 7-12 the Midland side. There were two places where all comings and goings could be seen – at the east end of platform 6 and the West end of platform 1. Platform 6 was by far the most popular and was packed to capacity with spotters. The railway authorities did not seem to mind so long as there was no interference with the smooth running of the station.

I can only recall one occasion when spotting was stopped, after a few idiots had misbehaved.

Platform 6 was not long enough to accommodate long trains and one peculiarity was that trains had to be 'set back' into a short siding. This was mainly to clear the points into platform 5. The first 2-3 coaches of expresses in platform 6 were out of the platform and the loco was under the Hill Street Bridge. My favourite spot was on platform 1. It was a spectacular sight watching a double headed black five and a Jubilee slipping as they laboriously started a heavy express out towards Monument Lane tunnel. Great clouds of smoke and steam would rise up into Navigation Street and Hill Street above the station.

Royal Scot 4-6-0 no. 46148. The Manchester Regiment awaits departure from platform 3 at Birmingham New Street in May 1960.

New Street was always grimy and smoky, especially on the Midlands side where the great arched roof added to the dismal atmosphere. This side produced the most interesting trains however and on a summer Saturday the platforms were crowded with holidaymakers. Relief trains were abundant, especially to and from the South and South West coast.

Motive power for these trains ranged from compounds and 2P's, double headed with black fives and Jubilees, to crabs and moguls released from freight duties. The trains followed each other in quick succession and were often being held at Saltley awaiting clearance. During the summer there was also a "Cadbury's Holiday Express" and a "Butlin" special. These sported a round headboard covering the smoke box door. Occasionally a B1 or B12 from York worked these trains.

There was a regular B1 working on the Immingham service – usually 'Mayflower 61379'.

The local services provided some interesting locos and stock, Coventry, Wolverhampton, Lichfield and Walsall trains were largely dominated by Stanier/Fowler 2-6-4 tanks from Aston, Walsall and Bushbury sheds. Derby, Gloucester, Worcester and Redditch trains produced 3F's, 4F's, Ivatt moguls, 2-6-4 tanks, black fives, compounds and 2P's.

BR Standard class 5 73044 awaiting the 'right away' for its southbound journey from Birmingham New Street June 1962.

The station pilot at New Street in the early days was the Webb Coal Tank 58960 which was always intriguing and provided many footplate rides. This was superseded by Monument Lane's tank 40108 which seemed to live in New Street.

Away from the loco side, the thing that really intrigued me was the long footbridge from the entrance in New Street to the Station Street entrance, with steps down each side to the platform. Each flight of steps had an archway with suspended gas lamps and halfway along the footbridge there was a signal box where the signal man's movements could be observed. There were no ticket barriers and access to all platforms was free. At the New Street entrance there was a roller blind which was enclosed in a glass case with all the train departures. This was wound on by two railway staff every so often as time progressed.

Queen's Drive divided the station in half and was always a bustle of taxis, trolleys and buses. I was always impressed by the rail recruiting centre, where in the window they had a perfect model of a Stanier Black 5.

Many happy hours were spent at New Street but it was never to compare with Snow Hill.

8. SNOW HILL STATION

Snow Hill Station was and still is located in Colmore Row, the main entrance across from the Great Western Arcade shopping centre. The entrance was magnificent with large stone arches, a broad concourse with the booking offices and the clock. The clock was large and double sided and was a designated meeting place – I bet it could tell a few tales. There were dozens of billboards with timetables and adverts for excursions to places around the country. There were also the Bookstalls and waiting rooms and a general air of spaciousness and tidiness. After passing through the concourse, one proceeded down one of two parallel broad corridors across the taxi ranks to the latticework ticket barrier. There was one for departures and one for arrivals. There were basically only two island platforms at Snow Hill with bays at the north end. The platforms were very wide and each had a full quota of waiting rooms, buffet, toilets etc. Platforms 1 and 5 were the main through platforms for northbound trains, with platform 5 handling the crack expresses. Platforms 7 and 11 were the main southbound platforms, with platform 7 handling the crack expresses. The bay platforms between 1 and 5 handled Dudley, Stourbridge and Worcester locals whilst the bays between 7 and 11 handled Wolverhampton and Wellington locals. Overriding all of this was the superb glass and steel roof.

A rare visitor to Snow Hill, Churchward 2-8-0 4702 raises the dust as it speeds through on a mixed freight. The scissors crossings are clearly visible. January 1960.

Local trains to Leamington, Banbury, Stratford and Oxford used mainly platform 11 which was also used by relief trains and parcels.

Local trains to Shrewsbury, Chester and relief trains used platform 1. There were two through lines between platforms 5 and 7 and much freight passed through Snow Hill unlike New Street. A scissors crossing half way along platforms 5 and 7 also enabled two short trains to be accommodated.

At the North end there were extensive carriage sidings and two or three locos were always at hand shuffling stock. The station pilot was very often a Tyseley Hall – Lady Margaret Hall being common.

At the South end the tunnel was at the platform end and the signal box was virtually inside the tunnel. There was also a siding and loading bay inside the tunnel which was horse shunted. I remember seeing the horse shrouded in smoke pulling a wagon into the bay. I believe the horse was stabled in an alcove in the tunnel.

Another entrance to the station was in Great Charles Street which passed underneath the station about halfway along the platform. This was a very dingy affair, always dark and cold. It gave access to the subway linking the two main platforms.

The station was magnificently spacious and was a delight to visit. The signal box at the north end always appeared to be balanced precariously on a stalk and the mass of hefty lower quadrant signals were a delight.

The northbound line dipped to a latticework girder bridge and the first signs of a loco arriving was the plume of smoke over the bridge, then the glint of copper as a Castle or King surged up the bank to the station. Of course occasionally it was a grimy Pannier, 0-6-2 or 28XX on a freight, but nonetheless, the sight was always exciting.

From the other direction there was a distant rumble as a train entered the tunnel growing to a crescendo as the train neared the platform. The excitement was not knowing what the engine would be until it burst through the thick smoke curling out of the tunnel.

As at New Street, many of the engines were seen over and over again but a visit to Snow Hill was always guaranteed to produce at least one 'foreign engine'. It could be a Bristol or Laira Hall or Grange, a Cardiff or Landor loco or a freight engine from almost anywhere. My notebooks record that I never visited Snow Hill without a 'cop'.

WD 2-10-0 locos were also occasional visitors and on very rare occasions one of the 47XX class. (see photo page 32).

Summer Saturdays produced a multitude of specials to the South coast, South West, south Wales and Central Wales. It was these that produced unusual locos, I once saw a Machynlleth Manor piloting a Grange on a train from Pwllheli. My favourite locos were the Castles and Kings mainly used on the 'Inter City', the 'Cornishman' and the 'Cambrian Coast Express'. The distinctive bark shaking the soot off the canopies as they blasted out of the station never failed to enthral me.

Footplate rides were difficult to obtain at Snowhill, although "cabbing" was easy enough. The main dodge was to ride to the carriage sidings on 'Lady Margaret' or 'Wyke Hall'.

Ex. Great Western chocolate and cream railcars worked from the bay platforms to Dudley, forerunners of the diesel multiple units (DMUs).

Snow Hill was always my favourite and I still cannot believe it has all but gone, although it is currently enjoying a revival (2006).

During a half day spent at Snowhill on 18th May 1959 I recorded Hall class 7908, 6971, 7912, 5927, 6952, 6974, 5987, 5917, 5957, 5927. King class 6001, 6020, 6009, 6010, 6017. Castle class 5042, 5045, 5018, 5070, 5045. Grange class 6861, 6866. Tank engines 4153, 4173, 4124, 5189, 5199,

4153, 4170, 8100, 5151, 5189, 8796, 9763. BR Standards 75006, 73032, 92230. Stanier 8F, 48415.

Mogul 6340. 7908 and 6001 were double headed.

During a half day spent at Snowhill on 15th July 1961 I recorded Hall class 5994, 5966, 6925, 4931, 5993, 5924, 4913. King class, 6020, 6016, 6012, 6025, 6022, 6017. Castle class, 5022, 7019. Grange class, 6861, 6856. Tank engines, 4179, 8796, 9763 4172, 6101, 4104, 4111, 4174. Moguls, 6385.

No diesels!

9. MOOR STREET STATION

There was one place where the comings and goings of New Street and Snow Hill could be witnessed together. Adjacent to Moor street the New Street lines dive under the Snow Hill lines and it is possible to clamber onto a wall where all lines could be seen. However it was a long drop down to the New Street lines and on reflection a very dangerous place to be. Nevertheless the best of both worlds could be had and in addition the local trains in and out of Moor Street could be seen. (Moor Street being the terminus of local trains to Leamington, Stratford and Lapworth). It

Precarious position! By balancing on a high wall the lines into Moor St, Snow Hill and New Street could all be seen. In these photographs taken within minutes of each other, a King is leaving Snow Hill tunnel and about to pass Moor Street while 45638 Zanzibar is entering New Street.

Small Heath station on 27th April 1963 with a FA cup semi-final train bound for Villa Park from Southampton. 8F 48417 leads rebuilt SR west country class 34039 'Boscastle'.

transpired that this was trespassing and after being threatened with the police a couple of times, this venue was abandoned. Nowadays the same spot is a car park and the New Street lines and Snow Hill Street lines can be observed without trespassing.

Preserved steam engines make the occasional visit to Snow Hill and recapture some of the old memories.

10. SMALL HEATH STATION

Small Heath station is on the ex GWR line from Snow Hill to London Paddington. It is the second station along the line from Snowhill and is between Bordesley and Tyseley stations. The Camp Hill freight only line crossed the Snow Hill-Small Heath line approximately half way between Bordesley and Small Heath. In the 1960s there were also many sidings adjacent to Small Heath station. It was an interesting place for "spotting". There were trains to and from Snow Hill and Moor Street, trains transferring from MR to WR regions, shunting movements and engines going to and from Tyesley shed. I have a detailed record of trains observed on 30th July 1960 as follows:

LOCO NO.	HOME SHED	DESCRIPTION	DIRECTION
D3958	84E	Shunting	–
9733	84E	Freight	Down
6858	84A	033	Up
5089	84A	V15 (London)	Up
7809	89A	F16 (Swansea)	Up
4902	81E	Local	Down
6877	85A	Light engine	Up
6001	84A	V16 (London)	Up
6866	84E	034	Up
7920	85A	Local	Down
4111	84E	Local	Down
5959	84E	F19 (Whitland)	Up
7338	85A	Light engine	Down
6391	82C	Light engine	Down
4919	81A	Z60	Down
4173	84E	Light engine	Down
9798	84E	Light engine	Down
9614	84E	Light engine	Down
5977	81D	036	Up
6877	85A	Light engine	Down
9753	84E	Freight	Up
75003	84E	Empty stock	Down
5046	84A	C33	Up
6956	84G	C76	Up
5906	81D	Local	Down
6017	84A	V02 (London)	Up
75003	84E	096	Up
4155	84E	Light engine	Down
6391	82C	045	Up
5037	81A	H05	Down
9614	84E	Freight	Up
75024	84E	Empty stock	Down
92233	84C	Freight	Down

LOCO NO.	HOME SHED	DESCRIPTION	DIRECTION
4938	84A	O44	Up
5322	86G	Light engine	Down
6861	84e	Light engine	Down
4998	81D	C82 (Paignton)	Up
6027	84A	V03 (London)	Up
5018	81D	O48 (Margate)	Up
7217	86A	Freight	Down
4941	81D	Express	Down
6847	86C	C84 (Minehead)	Up
73017	71G	B39 (Weymouth)	Up
6000	81A	M09	Down
7302	82D	J11	Down
5970	86G	Light engine	Up
4155	84E	Local	Down
4082	81A	V04 (London)	Up
5066	81A	Express	Up
5988	84C	V98 (London)	Down
5958	81A	Express	Up
4083	83A	H42	Down
5927	84E	"Cornishman"	Down
5032	83A	Express	
6929	84C	Freight	Up
5991	84B	Express	Down
4966	84B	Z75	Down
5947	87J	Express	Down
6975	84B	Express	Down
92210	86C	Light engine	Down
6349	84F	Light engine	Down
6834	82B	H35	Down
4083	83A	Light engine	Up
4155	84E	Light engine	Up
7302	82D	Light engine	Up

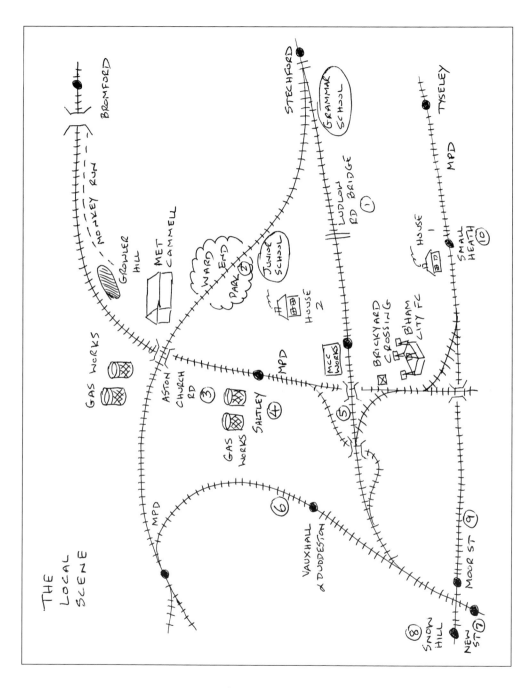

The Local Scene.

Chapter 4
FURTHER AFIELD

On looking through the thousands of locomotive numbers in the Ian Allan ABC books, it soon became obvious that in order to fill up some of the large gaps, journeys outside Birmingham area were needed.

TAMWORTH

A popular place much praised at school was Tamworth where there were high level and low level stations with trains every few "seconds". In fact this was not far off the truth and my first visit, travelling on the local train from Saltley was memorable.

The train was packed with spotters and on arrival at Tamworth we were 'escorted' to a field alongside the main London-North West line. Spotters were not allowed on the station. I was initially amazed at the vast numbers of spotters, the field was packed. As we were being escorted to the field two trains passed through at great speed on the low level and freight trundled across on the high level!

What a day that was – named expresses: The Royal Scot, Midday Scot, Red Rose, Mancunian, Comet, Irish Mail, and Devonian. Locomotives spotted included Patriots, Semis (Coronation Pacifics), Princesses, Jubilees, Royal Scots, Britannias, numerous freight locos, diesels 10000/10001 double headed and 10203. A hot day, bottles of pop, sandwiches – absolute heaven.

Tamworth became a regular spot and the jargon was soon picked up – the large down signal was known as the 'down clanger' and the up as the 'up clanger'. The smaller signal controlling the slow lines was known as "baby clanger". When the signals were pulled off by the signalman a loud cheer of "up clanger", "down clanger" or "baby clanger" would echo around the field. Trains could be seen approaching from the south a long way away and much guessing as to the type of loco was made. Some lads had binoculars or telescopes and would be the centre of attentions South bound trains could not be seen until they burst through the station, often at great speed.

Tamworth was also a good place to explore with the River Anker at the bottom of the field, plenty of farmland and animals. There was also the old line which used to link the high level with the low level, long since abandoned.

It was also possible to clamber up the bridge over the River Anker and come out between the up and down fast lines. A train roaring past at high speed only feet away was terrifying and exciting.

Station staff and police kept a watchful eye but I cannot remember any incidence of vandalism or any accidents. Occasionally we walked through the fields alongside the high level line to the water troughs just north of Tamworth. It was spectacular watching locos picking up water, on hot days we used to scramble down the embankment and enjoy a cool shower from a passing train!

There was a café in the station drive and the owners must have made a small fortune on Saturdays and in the school holidays!

The most popular return train to Birmingham was the 4.23pm from Tamworth and spotters were not allowed onto the platform until just before the train arrived. The unsuspecting passengers must have wondered what had hit them when a couple of hundred spotters joined their train! This train I remember was nearly always an Ivatt mogul and travelled to Birmingham via Whitacre which was then a large station.

Tamworth was heavenly and has been described as the "field of dreams". The field is now a park home site but it is still possible to walk down the field to the river. The "clangers" have been replaced by modern colour light signals, the café has been demolished to make way for a car park. It is still a good place to watch trains but not as frequent nor as exciting as in those halcyon days.

LICHFIELD TV

Lichfield Trent Valley was also visited occasionally, also having a high and low level. But the high level was very quiet with only a few trains. I remember at junior school one of my teachers a Mr Hesketh was a keen railway enthusiast. From his classroom could be seen Ward End park line. He kept a pair of binoculars in his desk and would tell us the numbers of locos passing through. He once organised a day out for us to Lichfield Trent Valley station and must have spent hours working out the times of all the trains. He gave us all a worksheet to fill in with a prize for the pupil who correctly identified the most loco types, wheel arrangements etc. I didn't win!

RUGBY

Rugby was one of the places which was also raved about and once I had convinced my parents that I was coming to no harm on these trips I was allowed to go. The train to Rugby passed through Coventry with its small shed and a few "cops" – Duck 8's and 2-6-2 tanks used on the Nuneaton-Coventry-Leamington branch.

On arrival at Rugby I was mesmerised by the mass of lines and train movements. The huge overall roof which is much the same today was also impressive. I remember we attempted to "bunk" the engine shed but were quickly thrown out. We then walked down several roads until we came to a patch of ground adjacent to the point where the ex Great Central line crossed the ex LNWR lines on a girder bridge.

This was a fabulous vantage point as all train movements could be seen except the line to Leicester. The locos seen here were the same as those seen at Tamworth with the addition of Birmingham trains and the Peterborough and Northampton service. Also of course was the ex Great Central line which was mainly freight with V2's, B1's, WD 2-8-0's and BR9F's. The freight trains were mainly coal trains and made a tremendous rumble as they crossed the girder bridge at high speed. There were a few passenger trains, locals hauled by N7 tanks and semi-fasts hauled by V2's and B1's. There was also the Sheffield to Marylebone Express, "The Master Cutler" usually hauled by an A3 Pacific.

Other memories of Rugby are the massive signal gantry and the testing station with all sorts of rumours as to which loco was "on test". There was always plenty of movement into and out of the shed with Super D's, Stanier Crabs, Ivatt tanks and moguls.

Rugby is like a ghost town now compared to how it used to be. The girder bridge and gantry have long gone, so have the loco shed and testing station and the mass of lines have been reduced. Only the station remains similar to how I remember it.

On a sunny day 3rd July 1959 I spent a day at Rugby and spotted the following engines: 44123, 45655, 43924, 58182, 45741, 45327, 45324, 44045, 43007, 48927, 58171, D3055, 48457, 42573, 45493, 44909, 45249, D212, 44836, 70047.

Rugby Shed: 44712, 46472, 48686, 44860, 48012, 48173, 42577, 48757, 42940, 48559, 44938, 45518, 58218, 49432, 43106, 43063, 48516, 44391, 42669, 49442, 49048, 12047, D2909. In store: 41909, 41902, 40016, 40003, 40007, 40054, 40070, 41162, 40050, 49266, 49112, 40042, 40051, 40053, 40045, 49442.

The field low level: 44715, 45106, 44716, 41227, 44863, 44836, 42061, 46126, 48601, 45093, 46108, 44714, 46154, 48544, 46204, 10000, (diesel). 44831, 48624, 44833, 45587, 48345, 70031, 48447, 41320, 48289, 48692, 42946, 44833, 46221, 46143, 44965, 46163, 46147, 46170, 45530, 44862, 45021, 46223, 46420, 46149, 45301, 45555, 45188, 46101, 45311, 46166, 46106, 48085, 45658, 49120, 43919, 45074, 42948, 45257, 70033, 45592, 45670, 45527, 45643, 45129, 46165, 10202 (diesel), 46132, 45574, 46240, 92250, 45686, 48312, 45680, 46238, 44870, 46252, 43001, 46205, 46243, 44766, 48411, D8002, D8003, 48723, 45737, 48090, 45064, 45039, 42964, 45599, 46234, 45510, 45531, 44752, 45740, 46161, 45146, 46160, 45109, 44773, 46156, 46115, 45556, 45540, 44321, 45191, 44840, 45050, 80082, 46445.

The field high level: 67741, 92067, 92010, 60890, 92090, 90520, 61085, 92072, 90065, 61369, 61116, 67789, 92043, 92092, 92095, 92012, 61156, 61298, 61843, 60879, 60831, 63592, 92093, 92032, 6979, 61368, 92070.

A good day 200 locomotives, 17 Royal Scots, 12 Jubilees, 4 Patriots, 2 Princess Royals, 6 Coronations, 3 Britannias and only 8 diesels!

CREWE

Mecca for train spotters that was Crewe. Especially if you were a fan of ex-LMS or LNWR and BR standard locomotives.

As everyone knows Crewe was, and still is, the meeting place of lines from London, Birmingham, Carlisle and Glasgow, Shrewsbury, Chester, Manchester, Liverpool and Stoke-on-Trent. There were massive marshalling yards South of Crewe, the works, North, South and Gresty Lane engine sheds.

A whole day was needed at Crewe to do it justice and it was usual to leave New Street at 8 am to arrive in Crewe just after 9am. The first task was to 'bunk' firstly Crewe South shed and then proceed past the football ground to the ex GWR shed at Gresty Lane. Crewe South shed housed mainly freight locos and was always guaranteed to provide a "cop". It was easy to bunk and I don't recall ever being caught. Gresty Lane was the ex GWR shed and had Halls, Panniers, Granges and an occasional Castle along with BR standards which had worked in from Shrewsbury. Then it was onto Crewe north with its Pacifics, Royal Scots Jubilees, Patriots and Brittanias. This was a difficult shed to bunk – the spotters way in was through a steel railing fence adjacent to the yard – if the fence had been bent! It was a very busy shed with constant moving of engines on and off – probably why the shed staff were so vigilant for trespassers!

One of the main features of Crewe station was the footbridge across the platforms at its northern end. This bridge gave a good view of train movements and was probably the most popular spotting place on the station. One end of the bridge led into Crewe North shed but this way in was almost impossible as it was in full view of shed staff.

Crewe was where many trains changed engines especially long distance expresses from Scotland to the south. Engines from Glasgow, Edinburgh and Carlisle would give way to engines from Crewe, Camden, Bushbury and Shrewsbury and vice versa. This was the place to see locos that never or rarely were seen near Birmingham. 46102 Black Watch, 46105 Cameron Highlander, 46222 Queen Mary, 46223 Princess Alice and if lucky a 'Clan' – all 10 of which were allocated to Glasgow or Carlisle.

Crewe works was the place to see a wide range of locos being built, under repair or awaiting scrapping. There was also the works shunters which rarely if ever left the confines of the works. Bunking the works was almost impossible as entry was through gates with a watchman. There were ways in but once in there was a high risk of being caught as there were fewer places to 'hide' from view and many workers who did not welcome intruders.

Visits were usually made on Sundays when the works would give guided tours for a small charge – I think there was one in the morning and one in the afternoon. Parties could also be booked in for a tour by writing to the works manager. Once inside the works spotters were expected to, and generally did, follow the guide. However there were parts of he works that were not included in the tour. The wily spotter would sneak away from the party to look into the paintshop, the condemned line and the works loco shed before rejoining the 'tour.' Parties were often a couple of hundred strong and it was easy to 'go missing'.

Locos inside the works were from everywhere and rare cops were to be had. Many engines were in pieces in various stages of repair and there was always debate about how much of a loco could be seen to make it an authentic cop. There were frames, boilers, cabs, wheels and tenders, all in different places, usually with the engine number painted or stamped on. Some purists argued that because parts were interchangeable the boiler marked 45000 might be a boiler from a different engine! Did you count both or none? I like to think that if I saw the cab side number then there would be enough other bits around to warrant writing the number down. After all it was the cabside number you wrote down at the lineside! There were always cops to be had with new locos under construction, once again there was debate about how complete a loco had to be before it could be spotted!

Even though Crewe is only a shadow of its former self, it is still an interesting place to visit.

Trip to Crewe 15th December 1963

5A (Crewe North)

44876, 70033, 78062, 45567, 41229, 46434, 44913, 46237, 46238, 44716, 45721, 70044, 44990, 70040, 44836, 42442, 44683, 45116, 45670, 70052, 44819, 45560, 45545, 46235, 70027, 70041, 44872, 70014, 41212, 45442, 44938, 44818, 44681, 70054, 70028, 47280, 42226, 46254, 61158, 44402, 78030, 70050

5B (Crewe South)

6925, 44901, 45093, 44670, 47648, 45033, 43001, 45370, 45058, 47677, 47530, 43113, 43024, 47384, 6830, 42943, 47400, 78055, 47399, 45741, 45733, 45302, 44443, 42970, 43026, 45067, 48559, 92015, 45372, 90606, 92174, 45586, 45263, 47494, 45248, 78031, 78036, 43026, 45067, 43034, 6841, 45391, 48258, 43049, 48246, 45092, 45275, 45639, 45200, 42798. 46503, 42771, 44988, 44882, 42213, 48672, 48495, 42796, 46524, 45081, 48643, 45239, 45535, 92095, 92157, 6860, 422778, 45259, 6863, 6823, 45024, 48667, 44666, 44906, 45494, 48194

Crewe Works

47380, 44373, 47646, 44405, 43957, 84023, 47615, 49395, 73128, 44686, 45491, 45327, 45139, 46452, 48255, 70025, 78028, 45072, 77002, 45736, 48632, 42355, 48219, 46448, 45406, 92090, 45019, 48415, 44714, 45006, 48418, 45308, 84021, 46142, 44762, 92178, 92233, 78064, 78000, 45345, 46465, 92024, 78033, 48412, 45296, 92011, 44958, 48614, 45316, 44932, 44900, 45280, 92128, 48705, 48128, 92183, 48000, 73127, 44856, 92081, 44726, 84013, 48411, 78023, 44714, 45438, 44919, 45375, 92067, 92114, 42785, 90338, 84024, 84022, 47658, 47597

Gresty Lane Shed

8798, 3664, 5019, 49044, 5063, 5919, 48737, 73132.

STAFFORD

Stafford may seem a strange choice of venue to go spotting but the reasons are straightforward. First it had the West Coast main line plus the line to Birmingham, secondly all the freight passed through – much of which could not be seen at Crewe as it went via the 'by pass'. Thirdly there was the excitement of trains passing through at speed – always a thrill and fourthly it was easy and cheap to get to!

I really enjoyed watching non stop trains come off the curve from the Trent Valley line – leaning over and whistling before hurtling through the station leaving steam, smoke, dust and swirling paper picked up in the draft.

The other interesting movement was trains coming off the Up fast line travelling to Birmingham. They would have to negotiate two crossovers and 'snake' their way across several tracks to reach their route. There was the added attraction of trains to and from Wellington and movement on and off the shed which was adjacent to the station.

WORCESTER

As mentioned in the first chapter, Worcester was visited with my father on his fishing trips. It later became a fairly regular spotting venue because of the range of locos which could be seen. It also gave opportunity to travel up the Lickey incline – always exciting!

I usually arrived at Worcester Shrub Hill, spotting as many engines as possible on the shed which was just outside the station – in case I could not get round the shed. Then I would 'bunk' the shed (fairly easy) and return to Shrub Hill. From Shrub Hill most of the trains into and out of Worcester could be seen easily. The exceptions were mainly freight trains from Hereford and South Wales which did not go through Shrub Hill. These could be spotted only with binoculars and to aid with this and other venues, I purchased a small pair second hand.

Worcester I remember as well for its line into Lea and Perrins sauce factory across the street and with semaphore signals controlling the road traffic. I recall the Pannier with the large upside down cone device on its chimney – spark arrester I believe. There was also the impressive bridge at Foregate Street and the girder bridge across the River Severn by the racecourse.

DERBY

Derby was a frustrating place to visit mainly because so many trains went around it! Its main attraction was the shed and works – both very difficult to get round without a permit. My visits were mainly restricted to open days – usually at the end of August. I have details of one such visit on 27th August as follows:

Derby shed

42089, 75049, 42238, 41726, D5080, D232, D5701/2/3/18, 10000, D5131, D3991/2, 42593, 47006, 44051, 42346, 73066, 43679, 42054, 44825, 42399, 42822, 43840, 42390, 45627, 73137, D212, 44865, 45619, 45598, 45618, 42541, 42486, 42146, 42587, 42161, 43985, D4, 46443,

47644, 47660, 48342, 45626, 46497, 43778, 43200, 45649, 45610, 45557, 44425, 44214, 43548, 47000, 43459, D3983/5/7, D3088, D3585, 46402, 48124, 48293, 44851, 44049, D3864, D5712/3, D2505, 47284, 73065, 43599, 90683, 44465, 43621, 61388, 45506, 44466, 41528, 47516, 42514, 43658, D234, 48301, 47630, 41712, 42229, 42376, 45618, 42066, 47661, 42524, 44235, 47441, 44289, 47638, 47533, 43599, 42181, 61348, 42568, 442101, 44344, 44334, 48390, 45651, 48132, 75059, 90497, 48250, 42798, 43033, 44945, 90719, 48748.

Derby Works

73031, 42422, 48364, 44215, 44534, 49045, 46116, 48272, 48057, 58305, 44434, 42763, 40396, 42756, 44966, D3569/86, 75059, 44033, 47643, 42332, D3775, 43435, 47458, 58144, 43639, 43359, 58209, 41123, 58158, 41157, 43843, 43174, 58157, 43771, 46499, 48156, 73003, 48001, 1000, D5704/ 11/16/17, 48356, 43510, 45097, 44753, 44841, 67775, 42486, 45088, 63610, 75009, 73016, 61740,61041, 92152, 61312, 73046, 42827, 67753, 45608, 42818, D5129/30/32/33/34/35/36/38/39, D3988/89/90/93/94/5/96/97, 73135, 71000, 42697, 73128, 44437, 42359, 47003, 73144, 48286, 47344, 42532, 42111, 42542, 42240, 42338, 42096, 44184, 42352, 48770, 48083, 42184, 42101, 42344, 43942, D11/12/13/14/15, 48356, D2906, D8009, D3066, D3374, 12087, 13118, 12033, 12051, ED2/3/6, 44066, 48523, 42210, 48096, 75055, 10800, 43394, 48083, 47203, 40489, 48388, 42067, 42288, 42384, 42069, 42102, 42074.

Derby was an exciting place with all the engine movements and named expresses "The Palatine", "The Thames-Clyde" and "The Devonian".

I was to travel much further afield, in fact the length and breadth of the country. Details of some of these travels are in later chapters.

Chapter 5

TRESPASS!

How many railway enthusiasts, train spotters, railway photographers can honestly say they have never trespassed onto railway property? Perhaps to secure a better position for a camera shot or a tape recording, to read the number of some locomotive hidden behind wagons or to 'visit' a loco shed without a permit or permission.

Trespass can be looked upon as foolhardy, dangerous, daring, lawbreaking or simply naive. Certainly there were many times when I was technically trespassing but assumed it was 'alright' because others were doing it. On reflection I would probably not have done so knowing now the possible consequences. However, my trespasses were always with a view to enlarging my number collection or broadening my knowledge of railways and their workings. I certainly never had any intentions of damaging property or person, nor of stealing anything – unlike much of the general vandalism, theft and violence which is part of today's life.

Visiting a loco shed without a permit from BR could be attempted in two ways – either to ask the foreman in charge for permission to 'look around' or to simply go in without permission and hope not to be caught. This latter method was known locally, perhaps nationally, as 'bunking'. E.g. Let's go and "bunk" Aston, I've just "bunked" Aston. Running away from the scene of trespass when spotted by a railway official was also known as 'doing a bunk'!

Shed foremen varied immensely in their attitude to spotters. Many readily gave their consent to 'visits' – usually with a word to be careful or very often "I haven't seen you". Some were hostile and used their extensive vocabulary to reject requests.

The difficulty was in deciding whether to ask permission or to "bunk". Once permission had been refused "bunking" became more of a risk as the foreman was probably on his guard and the consequences of being caught were greater.

Some sheds were easy to bunk and permission was rarely asked, others were almost impossible and a permit from BR was advisable.

Of the 'local' Birmingham sheds, Saltley (21A), Bournville (21C) and Monument Lane (21E) were all reasonably easy to 'bunk' or depending on which foreman was on duty to 'visit'. Aston was difficult to bunk with only one way in and that was past the office. There was a doorway in the wall in Longacre Rd and a stairway down to a small brick paved yard off which led a passageway into the shed. The procedure for bunking was to wait at the end of the passageway into the shed until it looked 'all clear' and then run down the passage ducking low past the office window and into the shed. Once in, the chances of being caught were low unless some 'vigilant' railway worker informed the foreman or told us to '.... off'.

In my experience most railway men in the shed turned a blind eye to 'spotters'. Once all the locos on shed had been spotted the reverse procedure was followed except that it was not as important not to be seen on the way out!

Saltley was easy to get into either through the canal fence at the side or directly into no. 1 Roundhouse from the entrance drive (avoiding the office.) Once in it was reasonably easy not to be caught except out in the loco yard which the foreman's office overlooked. Some deft dodging between rows of locos was needed to complete a tour of this large shed.

I had a set routine every Sunday morning after completing my paper round, of 'bunking' Saltley shed – there were always a few 'cops' to be had and always other spotters who had already been to Aston. They would tell me which locos were on shed at Aston and if I "needed" them I would go. This was a round trip of approximately 4 miles.

I did not visit the other Birmingham sheds frequently – Monument Lane and Bournville rarely had "foreign" visitors of interest and Tyseley was not easy to get to.

When Tyseley was visited it was quite difficult to 'bunk' – the offices were facing the main entrance from Warwick Road. The shed could be accessed from other directions all of which involved "trespass" – along the track from Tyseley station, through a woodyard and over a fence – none of which was easy. Once inside the shed the chances of being caught diminished and the Roundhouses, works and yard were a rich source of spotting, with many "foreign" locos on shed.

During my spotting days I visited nearly every MPD in Wales, England and Scotland – I never got to Ireland. I have many memories, some good and some which I would choose to forget.

I can certainly recall the largest and smallest MPD's – the largest was Stratford in London with an astounding 238 locos on shed (Sunday 8th March 1959).

The smallest and one of the most remote was Clee Hill in Shropshire. (see photo gallery). One loco was kept here for shunting in the quarry – the wagons were hauled by cable from the sidings at Ludlow. The shed was just that – a wooden shed reached across a field with the loco (0-6-0 saddle tank no. 1142) locked inside. The loco's number could be seen through the cracks in the timber shed sides. I assume the loco was also winched up and down the incline for repairs and servicing.

Other forms of trespass in the course of pursuing this hobby were usually to spot a loco hidden behind wagons or coaches. This often meant crossing running lines, ducking between wagons, climbing over obstacles – often to find the engine was one already previously spotted!

When I owned a camera I would often trespass to obtain a better picture, this happens nowadays of course but wearing a hi-visibility jacket seems to make it alright!

I can only recall one shed bunk where I was caught and became really scared. The shed was Copley Hill in Leeds during a coach tour of the area with the Bromford loco society.

A friend and I were caught by a foreman who locked us in his office and questioned us about how we had got there. Not wishing to jeopardise the coach party we said we had travelled by train, he asked us which station we had arrived at and where were our tickets. We then dug ourselves deeper into a hole and he went off to fetch the police, but not before he had taken my notebook and scribbled out all the numbers – I still have his handiwork! Fortunately, (or was it set up?) a driver came into the office and told us to scarper quickly. On leaving the shed the coach was nowhere to be seen. (half an hour had passed by). We walked up and down the road and were ready to make our way to Leeds station when the coach turned up! They had been driving round, passing the shed at intervals to see if we had been 'released'.

Chapter 6

HOLIDAYS

Once the railway bug had bitten, my life was tailored to suit and this included holidays. Family holidays were, as mentioned previously, nearly always at Rhyl in North Wales. Travel was by train and I would spend the time with notebook and pencil looking out of the window for locos. When Crewe approached it was frustrating to have so many locos on both sides – not knowing which side of the carriage to look out and not being able to write fast enough to note them all!

Once on holiday I tried to spend as much time as possible watching the heavy rail traffic on the North Wales coast line. I had to 'toe the line' more often than I wished and go with the family to the beach, the fair, shopping (we always went in a caravan and had to buy food daily) and other outings. However, I spent every opportunity to stand by the line side which ran alongside the caravan site (Happy Days site) 2 miles outside Rhyl at Kimnel Bay.

I was enthralled by the expresses (including the Irish Mail) the push pull shuttle with the headboard "The Welsh Dragon" and the numerous freight trains. The "Welsh Dragon" was I recall a tank engine with two or three coaches operating a push-pull service between Rhyl and Llandudno. Locos came in all shapes and sizes – mainly ex LMS together with BR standards and occasional WD 2-8-0's. Many excursion trains ran during the summer holidays bringing day trippers from around the country and it was not unusual to see 'crabs', '9F 2-10-0's and WDs on passenger trains. often very lengthy with 14 or 15 carriages in tow.

Another attraction at Rhyl was the steam miniature railway which ran from the fair 'Pleasure Land' around marine lake. I was fascinated by these miniature steam trains and I recall one was a 'King' class reproduction. The railway is still there (2006) and operated by diesel engines with occasional steam making an appearance.

I often went to Rhyl station and visited the shed near the end of the platform. Trains left from here to Corwen and Llangollen.

One holiday I remember very well was with my mates to Llandulas in North Wales staying in a caravan on Brough's Site in August 1964. The North Wales coastline ran alongside the site and we would dash to the fence when we heard a train coming. What the other holiday makers thought of this weird behaviour, god only knows! The holiday was a rich mixture of fun, sunbathing, playing football, train spotting and considerable drinking of alcoholic beverages.

During the week we managed to fit in a trip to Penrhyn slate quarry where we observed narrow gauge steam engines 0-4-0 "Glyder" and 0-4-0 "Nesta" at work.

We also caught the steamer from Llandudno for a day trip to the Isle of Man. While there we went to Douglas station and loco shed and were fortunate to see Beyer Peacock numbers 1, 10, 11, 12 and a diesel railcar. Unfortunately we didn't have time for a ride on the train.

One of the highlights of the week for me was meeting a young lady in the local pub and walking her back to her caravan. We kissed walking along the beach, my first real kiss – pow! Suddenly there was something else interesting in life! She lived in Stourbridge and I went to see her a couple of times after the holiday but it was not to last, especially when her boyfriend came home from the army!

I drove to Llandulas in my first car, a 1952 Morris Minor split screen side valve job. The two mates who had come with me and I decided to do a shed bash around Lancashire on the way home from the holiday!

Two incidents about this trip are implanted in my memory. Saturday night we couldn't afford to stay anywhere and decided to sleep in the car. I found a piece of waste ground near Wigan, parked up and we tried to sleep. As the driver I had the dubious comfort of the back seat. My friends took the very cramped front passenger and driver seats. It rained during the night and my friend in the passenger seat had the added discomfort of water dripping onto his leg through the leaking windscreen!

Sunday was hot, and the vehicle tax disc which was sellotaped onto the windscreen fell off. I told my mate to put it in the glove compartment. Later during the day I was pursued and stopped by a police motorcyclist. His sharp eyes had picked up the fact that there was no tax disc displayed. I asked my mate to retrieve the disc from the glove compartment – he put his hand in and pulled out a gooey mess: the remains of ½lb of butter which had been packed into the compartment had melted all over the disc! The policeman was able to decipher the gooey mess and allowed us on our way with a mildly amused rebuke.

During the Saturday we visited the sheds at Llandudno junction, Chester, Birkenhead, Edge Hill(Liverpool), Sutton Oak, Agecroft, Trafford Park, Newton Heath, Bury and Bolton. On Sunday we visited Springs Branch (Wigan), Lostock Hall, Blackpool, Fleetwood, Skipton,Low Moor, Ardesley and Wakefield. No wonder I was tired! On this bash I wrote down 460 engine numbers and only 'copped' eight! Such had been my train spotting exploits the previous years, I was down to my last couple of hundred locos still to be seen in the whole of Britain!

I was absolutely shattered as we neared home on Sunday evening and came very close to a fatal accident in Lichfield. Tiredness caused me to misjudge overtaking and we almost hit a Midland Red bus head on.

Another holiday with my mates was to Penally near Tenby on the Whitland to Pembroke Dock branch. (July 1963). We hired a camping

Camping coach at Penally ex GWR 9676. Left to right 'neighbour', Pat Sheehan, Roger Hinton, Graham Gwynne.

coach located alongside Penally station which in itself made the holiday unique. The coach was well equipped and I remember the sumptuous breakfasts we enjoyed every morning the smell of 8 lots of bacon and eggs being cooked must have set the locals mouths watering!

We all travelled by train to Penally but not all together and I remember I had a circular tour ticket. This enabled me to travel outwards via the Central Wales line and return via Cardiff and Newport. I have details of this journey in my notebook as follows:

"Leave Snow Hill on 27th July pulled by 'County' 1014 to Shrewsbury. Change at Shrewsbury and then pulled by 48761 'Consol' 2-8-0 to Llandilo where I changed again and was pulled by 'Collett' 0-6-0 2287 to Carmarthen. I 'bunked' the shed which had 23 locos on including 82031 (Machynlleth), Castle 5087, Standards 73037 and 75009, Manor 7826 and Castle 4081 in store. There was one diesel on shed D6855 (class 37)".

I then travelled to Penally via Whitland pulled by prairie tank 4132.

The return journey was on 3rd August and I was pulled by 2-6-0 7332 to Whitland and then by Manor 7815 to Llanelli. I am unsure of how I got to Swansea but was pulled from there to Cardiff by Castle 5051. I went to Barry and Ferndale (both DMUs) and then back to Cardiff. In the early hours of Sunday 4th August I travelled to Newport behind Hall 7913 – visited the sheds and then caught a DMU to Hereford – stopping to visit the shed and finally to Birmingham on another DMU.

More details and incidents of this return journey are outlined later in this chapter.

Penally was on the branch from Whitland to Pembroke Dock and although there were not many trains we quickly got to know some of the railwaymen. I was privileged to ride on the footplate of a class 45XX from Penally to Pembroke with a tape recorder to record the journey. There was not much 'spotting' to be done during the holiday we simply enjoyed the warm sun, the beach and the local pubs.

There were two pubs in Penally – a large one on the main road and a much smaller one tucked away up a side street "The Cross". We quickly made friends with the very elderly, disabled landlord and in next to no time he allowed us to serve behind the bar while he relaxed and enjoyed the dubious company of eight young 'Brummie' lads. I don't know who enjoyed themselves more, us or him but he was genuinely sorry when we had to leave.

I recently went back with my wife and son (1999). The Cross is still there, much modernised, larger, gaming machines and bar meals – a disappointment. A new road cuts across where the camping coaches stood but the station is still there. I had a pint and reminisced, the sound of a steam engine, the lads singing 'twist and shout' as we walked along the beach from Tenby, the elderly landlord who was so tolerant of eight Brummie lads. Was that a GWR whistle I heard?

The spotting started in earnest after the holiday on the return from Penally. I travelled back via Swansea, Cardiff, Newport and Hereford and visited as many sheds as possible over Saturday and Sunday. Saturday afternoon and evening I "bunked" the sheds at Llanelli, Neath and Duffryn yard. I went to Radyr, Barry, Ferndale and Cardiff East Dock sheds before having a pie and a pint in a pub just outside Cardiff station.

I then went to the station waiting room and attempted to get some sleep on a bench. I was awoken in the early hours by a policeman who was questioning several 'dossers' about why they were there. My explanation and a valid train ticket allowed me to stay until my train to Newport. At Newport – it was early and still dark – I walked the long walk to Newport Pill shed. I was carrying my faithful tape recorder and a rucksack (my suitcase had been sent on the train to Birmingham!) Once again I was stopped by a policeman who gave me a real grilling, particularly about the tape recorder, thinking I had committed a burglary and stolen it! After convincing him of my innocence he wished me well. I thought he was going to ask for my non-existent shed pass.

I went on to 'bunk' Newport pill and Ebbw Junction sheds, an eerie experience in the dark. I then caught my train to Birmingham a cross country DMU with 'cats whiskers' at the front. I took time out in Hereford to visit the shed and then caught another train to Birmingham, I slept most of the way back!

I have mixed memories of two holidays abroad when seven of my Bromford loco club mates and myself decided to holiday in Spain (1964) and Italy (1965). Being railway enthusiasts the only way we would consider getting there of course was by train! In the early 1960s the holiday industry was just getting started and was a different package to what is expected nowadays! In 1964 we booked a "package" with Lyons Holidays which involved a thirty two hour train journey from London Victoria to Callela "Costa Brava". We stayed in London overnight at a friend's home and spent some time at Waterloo Station catching the last years of the SR Pacifics. Our train was a through train from Calais, steam hauled for the first part of the journey and then a mixture of electrics and diesels. The overnight journey through France was spent trying to sleep on rock hard 'couchettes'. At Port Bou on the French/Spanish border we were amazed as the carriages were lifted and the bogies changed to a different gauge!

The Hotel Tres Banderas in Callela on the Costa Brava was small and basic but comfortable and friendly – we were among the first "Brits" to stay there. The food was Spanish with no concessions to English taste but we washed it down with plenty of cheap plonk and paid many visits to the loo! The resort was still being developed and the roads were earth tracks which turned to rivers of mud when we had a fierce storm. I recall we caught a local bus to a village in the hills, we shared the bus with locals, chickens and a goat!

There was a "mini" bullfight being held in the village and volunteers were being called for. Laced with "el cheapo vino" I elected to be a 'matador' and duly entered a small bullring armed with a red cape and a wooden sword. A baby bull appeared, took one look at me, clawed the ground and charged. All I remember next is being picked up by two Spaniards and carried to safety behind a barrier. My sandals were spread one each side of the bullring and the bull was chewing one of them. The large bruise on my thigh lasted for a month, however I have had many drinks telling the tale.

The electrified railway line ran from Callela to Barcelona along the seafront and we travelled into Barcelona sightseeing. No steam trains, all electric and diesel but what a fabulous station, just like a Cathedral. During the holiday we had our photograph taken in the hotel bar and this was used in the Lyons 1966 holiday brochure, which I still have – fame indeed!

The holiday in Italy was an interesting railway journey, particularly as it went through Switzerland. The only steam engines we saw were in Milan with a couple of shunters in the freight yards. Our train took us to the outskirts of Rimini from where we were transferred to the Hotel King in Cattolica. It was an enjoyable holiday which included a visit to the principality of San Marino – a hair raising coach journey up a mountain.

Railway wise the holiday was uneventful, apart from the long journey there and back. none the less it was something which is impossible to do nowadays with no through trains available from London to Spain or Italy.

Chapter 7

PHOTO GALLERY

Leaking steam profusely Fowler 0-6-0 3F 43812 banking a freight train up Camp Hill bank at Landor Street on 15th October 1960.

Bromford Loco Club Scotland tour May 1961 0-4-0 class Y9 68101 with makeshift saddle tank tender! Photographed at Dunfermline shed.

Bromford Scotland trip 10th June 1962. 2P 40615 and Jubilee 45621 Northern Rhodesia at Glasgow Corkerhill shed. Impressive neat and tidy shed yard!

Modified Hall 6965, Thirlestaine Hall and BR 9F 92227 under the footbridge at Cardiff Canton shed 1st May 1961. The footbridge was a great vantage point to watch engine movements.

On the same day Britannia 70023 Venus in spotless condition awaits her next duty code 102.

The smallest shed I visited, Clee Hill. Inside was 0-4-0 saddle tank 1142 which could be seen through the gaps in the woodwork as the shed was padlocked. May 1961.

One of the largest sheds was Carlisle Kingmoor. BR Clan Pacific 72008 Clan MacLeod was photographed on 11th June 1962.

Another large shed was my 'home' shed of Saltley. 8F 2-8-0 48538 is outside no. 1 roundhouse (3 in total) next to the sand drying kiln. Also in the picture is Class 31 diesel and brake tender. Date unknown. Brian Dunckley.

Winter at Annesley shed with 63711, 84007 and 84027 stored between stacks of coal. Clambering over the coal to 'spot' these locos was a hazardous business! 18th November 1962.

My daughter did a course in photography and as part of a 'perspective' project took this photo of Moor Street Station on Birmingham in 1989. The station was still in use as a terminus after the closure of Snow Hill and before the 'new' Moor Street station was built. The terminus has now been refurbished and awaiting reopening (August 2006). Photo by Dawn Brueton.

Branch line wanderings took me along the Severn Valley line. Buildwas Junction is where the line crossed the Wellington to Much Wenlock branch. June 1960.

The local scene. This is Monument Lane shed on a misty morning 31st March 1961. 4F 0-6-0 44506 and 4-4-0 Compound 40936 are both in store. Roy Baker.

Fowler 'Crab' 2-6-0 42765 at Bewdley Severn Valley Railway awaiting departure for Kidderminster at the enthusiasts weekend September 2004. In the background is 'black five' 45110.

Ivatt 2-6-0 mogul 43046 at Bromford Bridge station on 22nd March 1961. These locos were known as 'flying pigs' with their high running board and ugly appearance.

Brough's caravan site at Llandulas in North Wales where 'the lads' enjoyed a week's holiday. The North Wales main line is in the background.

Bromford Loco. Club trip to Scotland in May 1962. The coach drivers pose in front of Flight's Tours TOB 377. An AEC with Burlingham "Seagull" body. This was near Perth.

Stanier Pacific 46238 City of Carlisle on Crewe North Shed May 1962.

Ex Lancs and Yorks 0-6-0 52218 one of Crewe Works shunters May 1962.

*M7 0-4-4 no. 30107 looking very smart at Bournemouth Shed in August 1960.
The author was pulled by this loco on the branch line to Lymington to board the
ferry for the Isle of Wight.*

*Un-named Patriot 45544 at Crewe Works awaiting a visit to the paint shop.
11th December 1960.*

Gresley Pacific A3 60044 Melton at Doncaster Shed on 26th November 1961.
Fitted with German style 'blinkers'.

Gresley K4 2-6-0 61998 MacLeod of MacLeod in store at Thornton Shed
21st May 1961.

A line of stored engines at Bo'Ness 21st May 1961. From front are ex-Caledonian 67269, J88 68325 and more ex-Caledonians 57287, 57338, 57466, 57229.

BR Standard Class 5 73041 banks a heavy holiday train out of Weymouth up Upwey bank. Summer Saturday 12th August 1960.

Ambition realised! The author opens the regulator on 8F 48773 during a Severn Valley Railway driving course.

Other side of the footplate! Firing the same engine during the course. October 2003.

The last number in the book! 92250 at Newport Ebbw Junction shed on 22nd May 1960. Fitted with a German Geisle ejector on the chimney.

The last steam engine built. 92220 Evening Star at Cardiff Canton on 1st May 1961.

Black five 45158 Glasgow Yeomanry one of only four named out of 842. Photographed at Polmont shed May 1961.

A view from the footbridge at Cardiff Canton Shed with the fireman of Britannia 70024 Vulcan pulling coal forward. 1st May 1961.

Smokebox close up of ex Caledonian 56376 in store at Grangemouth Shed 21st May 1961.

Aston Church Road (chapter 3) as it is now. The Camp Hill banking engines waited in two sidings now lifted nearest the camera. A class 66 passes. Note in the distance Saltley Gasworks being demolished. June 2005.

The 'Monkey Run' is still there on the right between the railway and the road in this June 2005 picture. Washwood Heath sidings on the left. Bromford Bridge is dwarfed by the new Spine Road flyover.

Steam to spare! Coronation pacific 46243 City of Lancaster and Black five 44876 wait in the centre roads at Carlisle Citadel station July 1960.

Dave 'dozy' Cole celebrates spotting his last Jubilee 45665 Lord Rutherford of Nelson at Corkerhill shed Glasgow 22nd May 1961.

Stratford shed London, the largest I visited. On 12th June 1960 B17 'footballer' 61660 Hull City stands in the yard.

South Wales sheds on a Sunday were deserted. Pannier 4685 rests quietly at Aberbeeg before its recommencement of work on Monday shunting coal wagons. 1st May 1961.

A selection of excess fares to supplement railrover tickets. Worcester to Bromyard, Matlock to Buxton and Rowsley to Millers Dale are included.

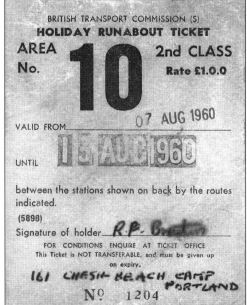

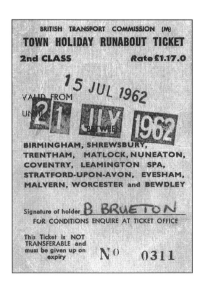

A selection of Runabout tickets used by the author in the early 1960s.

A selection of tickets from the author's collection.
Note the LMSR Vauxhall and Duddeston and the GW Rlwy Bordesley tickets
which were still being issued in the 1960s!!

In 1961 the Bromford Railway club did a tour of Scotland. This tram was photographed near to the Youth Hostel in Glasgow May 1961.

Templecombe shed on the Somerset and Dorset line with 2P 40563 outside its home depot. August 1960.

Schools class 30910 Merchant Taylors pauses at Yeovil Junction with a Westbound train in August 1960.

Another Schools Class 30934 St. Lawrence at Bricklayers Arms Shed on 12th June 1960.

Superb photo of 4F 44168 at Water Orton Junction taken from the signalbox by Roy Baker in June 1962. Roy Baker.

The author poses alongside 14xx tank 1432 at Oswestry shed in 1960.

Bromford, the 'monkey run', Nechells gasworks 2005. Compare this with photo on page 101 taken from a similar viewpoint.

'Grange' 4-6-0 no. 6867 Peterston Grange pauses at Evesham station heading towards Oxford on 1st June 1963.

Sunshine breaks the gloom of New Street Station as Jubilee 4-6-0 no. 45725 Repulse awaits departure with a South bound train on 18th March 1961.

The 3.35pm Leicester-Birmingham DMU calls at Bromford Bridge on race day, 3rd April 1961. Roy Baker.

Jubilee 4-6-0 no. 45705 Seahorse arrives at platform 3, New Street Station with an excursion train, 18th March 1961.

Fowler 4F no. 44131 is framed by semaphore signals as it approaches Bromford Bridge with a long freight train.

Chapter 8

ANIMAL ENCOUNTERS

During my travels around the country there were several incidents involving animals particularly dogs, which provided moments of terror, panic and some amusement.

I recall a visit with the Bromford loco club to Wadebridge shed in Cornwall. It was an overnight trip and Wadebridge shed was reached in the early hours of Sunday morning. It was pitch black and deadly quiet until a dog, disturbed by these "night raiders" started barking – immediately setting off a chorus of other dogs. The peace was shattered, lights came on in local houses and shouts were made. Fortunately Wadebridge shed was quickly visited with just 4 locos on shed and a hasty departure was made!

A dog was to play a more threatening part during a visit to Corkerhill shed in Glasgow when a large dog (Alsatian I think) was let loose by one of the shed staff. One of my mates had his trouser leg badly torn and his rucksack ripped off his back – sandwiches scattered everywhere. Luckily the dog stopped to eat them! I have never moved so fast before or since!

The final dog story is of the opposite nature. It was a visit to Tyne dock shed in the north east. The shed was a long walk from the station. My mate and I were walking around the shed with no problem when we became aware of a third member of our party! A small brown and white dog was following us around! On leaving the shed the dog followed and we suddenly realised we had made a friend! We tried in vain to shoo it away – walked back into the shed hoping it would go back to its owner or home. It did 'disappear' for a short time but as soon as we walked off it reappeared.

There was no-one about to ask whose it was nor any way of securing it to anywhere. We placed a pile of custard cream biscuits on the floor which the dog immediately tucked into and then we scarpered. The dog must have devoured the custard creams and then followed our scent. We had barely run a few hundred yards down the street and the dog was behind us again. We had a train to catch and decided to head for the station. The dog dutifully followed us all the way and would I am sure have boarded the train had it not been for one of the station staff apprehending it. I will always remember the doleful look the dog gave us as we left – I wonder if it ever got back home – did it only follow train spotters?

Sheep while not threatening, always amused me and on Sundays sheds in the Welsh valleys were invariably invaded by 'woolly backs!' Welsh valley sheds were fascinating places on Sunday. The engines were all quiet – just the occasional sizzle, 'drip drip' or clunk of metal cooling down.

Invariably the sheds were deserted – everyone off at the church, the social club or just relaxing at home. Sheep wandered around the shed – jumped across pits, scattered as we approached or just stood looking – almost saying who are those idiots rushing around writing down engine numbers!

The final animal encounter I recall could have had severe consequences. I was on a caravan holiday with my parents at Goodrington near Paignton in Devon. Access to the beach from the caravan site was over a sleeper crossing with steps up and over a wall each side of the Paignton to Kingswear railway line. One evening returning from the beach on a very warm day there was a snake curled on the top step, eyes open, forked tongue moving in and out. I looked around for a long stick (a very long stick!) to try and move it. My father said its only a harmless snake, grabbed it and threw it into the grass. When I looked it up in my Observers Book its zigzag markings were clearly those of a poisonous adder! I think the snake was too surprised by my father's quick action to strike out.

Patriot 45541 Duke of Sutherland poses outside Huddersfield shed in May 1960.

Chapter 9

FARE DODGING

Yes I admit it, occasionally I did not pay my train fare – sometimes deliberately, sometimes simply because I was not asked to pay.

I can recall several experiences – probably the best fare dodge known to Birmingham spotters was the Leamington Spa 'dash'. All one had to do was buy a platform ticket at Snowhill station and then board a Paddington bound express – first stop Leamington Spa. Invariably hauled by a 'King' it was an exciting high speed dash. On arrival at Leamington we could stay there for a time or catch a Birmingham-Wolverhampton express back behind another 'King'. On arrival back at Snowhill one could saunter nonchalantly around or catch another Paddington bound train. Tickets in my experience were never inspected between Snowhill and Leamington and vice versa. It was possible to spend all day going backward and forward to Leamington but the novelty soon wore off!

A similar 'dodge 'could be done between New Street and Coventry but it was more risky and not so certain about the inspections.

I did not make a habit of fare dodging it was usually when I was genuinely short of money. I was caught twice and the second time was scary enough to put me off. I was spotting at Shrewsbury and fancied a trip to Crewe but couldn't afford it. A fellow spotter at Shrewsbury told me it was easy as the tickets were not inspected on the train Crewe being a closed station.

I duly boarded a train for Crewe and after Wem an inspector came round! I hastily told him I had boarded the train at Wem and had not had time to buy a ticket. Liar! He said he had seen who had got on at Wem and I certainly did not. I buckled under his interrogation and told him I intended to get a ticket at Crewe. He told me to pay the fare to him and of course I couldn't. He took my name and address and on arrival at Crewe handed me to another railway official who questioned me further and gave me a real dressing down. I was then put on the next train back to Shrewsbury and told I would hear from the railway police.

My next few weeks were lived in fear of the postman or a knock on the door. However I never did hear anymore but it was certainly a deterrent!

The first time I was caught when I wanted to go to Exeter and paid for a day return to Weston-Super-Mare intending to pay an excess and stayed on the train to Exeter. There was no ticket inspection and when I got to Exeter I walked off the platform into the shed and came out into the street. I then caught a bus to Exmouth junction and successfully "bunked" it. Having "got away with it" on the outward journey I tried my luck on the return trip. However a ticket inspector came round and I duly had to pay the excess fare. The inspector did not give me a dressing down but just accepted my explanation about not having time to get a ticket at Weston or Exeter.

There have been numerous occasions when I have not had a ticket because I either was in too much of a rush to catch a train, there was no ticket office or I had extended my journey. On many of those occasions I have not been asked for a ticket.

The Author looks out from the cab of 'Dukedog' 9005 at Oswestry shed on the 19th July 1959.

Chapter 10

MISCELLANEOUS MEMORIES

I have many memories either directly linked to train spotting or railways or which relate to a time, a place or an era. I have vivid memories of the smoke, grime and industry in Britain in the late 50s and early 60s. Railways generally, especially in large conurbations were accompanied by industry and housing.

My general overriding memory is of rows of terraced houses, cobbled streets, washing lines hung across streets. Corner shops, grubby looking pubs, large factories, noise, smells, smoke and fog!

Who can forget the real fogs – yellow sulphuric, smog, choking, and long lasting. I recall at least one spotting trip by coach where the return journey (fog seemed to descend early evening) was a nightmare. Often one of us would have to walk in front of the coach, especially at road junctions and islands to guide the driver. People had torches and flares to help but journey times would be greatly extended.

I also recall the noise and smells of heavy industry – now virtually disappeared. Many loco sheds, sidings, and points were there to serve a large industrial area: Sheffield Grimethorpe (an apt name), Millhouses at Rotherham, Staveley with its steelworks, Hartlepool and Stockton with the chemical factories and docks, Frodingham with its steelworks and many more. The sense of power, the noise, and the smells. Staveley was a classic where the little 0-4-0 tanks were used to shunt around the steelworks seven days a week. Visits to the works were 'unofficial' but once inside, the sight and sound of steelmaking – sparks, smoke, and noise were both frightening and fascinating.

The numerous coalfields around the country (now virtually disappeared) were also served by the railways and were fascinating places to visit. My fondest memories are of South Wales with its valley lines – each one serving several mines. Each valley ran virtually parallel to the next one, separated by a ridge of hills. Each was accessed by a road climbing up and down the hills! I would like to have journeyed up the valleys by train in the days of steam but only managed a couple of them (to Merthyr and Treherbert). Obviously for maximum train spotting locos on shed, they had to be visited on a Sunday.

The Welsh valleys were fascinating – steep roads descending into the valleys – slag heaps adding to the mountain scenery – sheep – rows of terraced miners houses and the singing! Everything seemed to close down on a Sunday and a loco shed was usually unstaffed, sheep wandered around and the only sounds were the hissing of the engines, dripping water and the Welsh voices from the local chapel! Everywhere there were signs of coal-wagons full of it, stockpiles of it, pit head machinery and the slag heaps.

A scoot around the engine shed and then it was off to the next valley, up and down the hills. The coach drivers cursed these trips and I recall one occasion during a long descent into a valley, the coach brakes became very hot and were smoking. The driver had difficulty in stopping – fortunately there was not much traffic about!

Some of the loco sheds were very small with 5/6 engines – Ferndale, Dowlais Cae Harris, Rhymney and Ferndale spring to mind.

Typical Welsh Valley shed Sunday 2nd September 1961. Pannier 9457 at Duffryn Yard shed in the shadow of the hills.

Docks were another fascinating place – Southampton, Cardiff, Liverpool, Immingham, Grimsby, Hartlepool and of course Barry.

Cardiff docks were a real maze of railways, roads and waterways. I recall my first visit, I travelled with a mate to Cardiff by train and we caught a bus into dockland armed with a map showing all the sidings etc. The idea was to spend the day walking around trying to spot as many of the allocation of locos to Cardiff East dock shed as possible. We found the shed which was almost empty and spent hours getting lost, being bawled at by dock security, feeling threatened by the roguish looking dock workers. However we spotted many locos (and boats) and I can still see the cranes, the movement, the smell of oil and the black water. I am not sure if we went into the notorious Tiger Bay area but I didn't see or hear Shirley Bassey! On another visit to Cardiff docks a few years later, this time by coach on a Sunday, it was a totally different scene. Canton shed was being rebuilt for diesels and its fleet of locos had been reallocated to East dock, Castles, Britannias, Halls etc. along with the dock locos. The dock area seemed smaller, many wharves were out of use, and sidings were lifted or overgrown. I felt saddened as I was to continue to do so, and still am when I return to places which have such vivid memories.

USA tank 30063 outside Southampton Docks shed August 1960.

Southampton docks, was, I was assured a difficult place to get into – I recall the high walls and official buildings around it – the security guarded gates. Not surprising really with its high profile – the base for Cunard and other large shipping companies. Here were the USA tanks, ugly looking beasts but the spotter who had seen them all was envied by his mates.

My first visit was when I was on holiday with my parents at Weymouth. I had a rail rover ticket and decided to try and get into the docks – no problem! I must have touched lucky because I walked into one of the gates waiting to be challenged but was not and spent a happy couple of hours. I found the shed which only had two locos on and then wandered around spotting several others and the Canberra cruise liner! I recall other visits with permits (coach trips) and another 'bunked' visit with no problems.

Liverpool has two stirring memories – one was a school visit when I must have been nine or ten years of age. I remember the overhead railway and steam engines along the road underneath it! The coach had to stop to allow a train to cross in front of it! I never travelled on the overhead railway but do recall the girder bridges, the supports and the rumbling of the trains. The other memory is Bank hall shed – one shed I visited several times but never got round. The yard could be seen from an over bridge but the entrance and the vigilance was such that I never got into it. The minute 0-4-0 dock shunters 51218 and 51221 were stabled here.

Immingham I recall for its rows and rows of oil tanks and its fleet of 9F's which were difficult to 'spot' in the Midlands. There seemed to be miles of pipe work like a giant 'plumb crazy' game. Just down the road at Grimsby the smell of fish dominated the atmosphere and I remember lots of wood slatted buildings which I presume were fish warehouses. In 1992 as I passed through Grimsby by train en route to Cleethorpes the smell was still there!

Hartlepool sticks in my memory for its rows of cranes and its loco shed next to the sea. On one visit the sea was very rough and waves were seemingly about to crash over the sea wall into the shed.

Barry – where would the present day preservation societies be without Barry and Dai Woodham? My first sight of Barry was a visit with the Bromford Loco society of South Wales sheds. I have vivid memories of rows and rows of coal wagons, cranes, ships and coal 'tipplers' along the coast at Pensarn and Barry. Barry shed was at the road junction for Barry Island. Between the shed and the Island, more lines of wagons, to be followed in later years by lines of redundant steam engines.

I recall my first visit to the 'graveyard' – it was during a day trip by train to Barry Island with my wife and children, a fellow enthusiast and his wife and children. While our wives and daughters sunbathed on the beach, my friend and our sons walked along the rows of engines. I was moved to tears – especially reading the chalked and painted messages such as "don't let me die" with faces and teardrops on smoke box. There were lots of enthusiasts cleaning "their locos", salvaging parts and taking photos – I did myself.

Top: Dai Woodham's scrapyard at Barry circa 1983. My son, on left, was moved by the 'graveyard' even though he was born after the end of steam on BR! Bottom: By contrast 0-4-2 tank 1447 ex Caerphilly Works at Radyr shed 1st May 1961.

Chapter 11

SOCCER AND STEAM

My father took me to my first football match – it was an evening game, Birmingham City against Carlisle in the quarter final of the FA cup! The year was 1955. It was memorable because just after we went into the ground we got separated and with a crowd of 50,000 plus it was "needles and haystacks". I stayed close to the entrance – cowering – not seeing any of the match until my father found me at half time, cuffed me round the ear and vowed never to take me again!

From that day, in spite of the bad experience I became a 'Blues' supporter! So where does the steam come in? Not so much steam as smoke – from the railway end of St. Andrews the Blues home ground. Adjacent to the railway end was the Camp Hill bank where freight trains travelling from Saltley direction to all points west would be climbing, usually assisted by one or two banking engines (usually 3F 0-6-0's). As the train passed the ground the fireman on the engines would make every effort to create as much smoke as possible. No matter which way the wind was blowing the smoke would drift across the football pitch!

At times it was so bad it was impossible to see who was kicking what! It was particularly impressive during an evening game with the floodlights on – especially if it was a bit misty anyway. A huge roar would come up from the crowd when the game was obliterated! It would be interesting to know if complaints were made and whether firemen were ever reprimanded for their mischief!

Football and train spotting amalgamated and fortunately most of my mates were Blues fans – or at least interested in the game. The two hobbies were often combined and we would travel to matches around the country usually by trains – and if there was a shed or two to visit – so be it!

I remember the Boxing Day football excursion to see Manchester City v Blues – lots of drink, raucous singing but usually good natured and with no trouble. Arriving at Manchester on a snowy boxing day – only to be told the game against Manchester City had been called off. A quick

94

discussion and off on the train to Oldham to see Southport get hammered 11-1 in a snowstorm!

There were several days out in London to see Blues at Chelsea, Fulham, Tottenham, Orient, QPR and Arsenal. Most of these were by train either into Euston or Paddington. Wherever possible a visit to one or more sheds would be made – Old Oak, Willesden, Stewart Lane, Nine Elms, and Camden.

Time was limited as many of these trips were one day – 'soccer specials'. However occasionally we would spend the weekend in London staying at a 'friend of a friends' flat – sometimes eight or ten of us sleeping where we could find a space! This usually meant spending Sunday shed bashing – sometimes all together – sometimes splitting up to visit sheds where we were likely to find 'cops'.

Our love of football eventually led to us forming a team and joining the South Birmingham Sunday League. What did we call ourselves? 'Western Star' after Britannia 70025! We played for three seasons doing quite well and then folded due to other commitments.

A visit to Eastleigh Works in August 1961 found Adams 4-4-2 tank 30584 awaiting repair before returning to duties on the Lyme Regis branch.

Chapter 12

SCHOOL AND STEAM

As mentioned elsewhere my junior school was Nansen road from where it was possible to see the New Street avoiding line through Ward End Park. Not very exciting except when diversions were in operation. As mentioned previously Mr Hesketh was my teacher and also a train spotter. He would use binoculars to spot trains going through Ward End Park and then write the numbers on the blackboard for us.

I recall he organised a day trip out for the whole class to Lichfield Trent Valley station! He had spent time preparing a timetable and destination for all the trains that we would see which he handed out to everyone. We had to fill in the engine number and passing time of each train and work out if the train was on time, early or late. This was probably a "mathematical" means of justifying the trip to the head teacher. It was a great day out, hot and sunny. We caught a train to Lichfield city and walked across some fields to Lichfield Trent Valley. The whole class seemed to enjoy the trip except for one lad who fell into (or was he pushed?) a cowpat on the way back!

However when I gained a place at Saltley Grammar school the immediate attraction was the main Birmingham-London (Euston) railway line which ran alongside the school.

The school had an excellent reputation with good exam results, good sport record, particularly rugby and cricket, and a very strict uniform policy. I was in awe of the teachers with their gowns and (sometimes) mortar boards. I was scared stiff and felt like a fish out of water – it took me almost the whole of the first year to 'settle in' – after which I did very well (more of this later).

I walked from home to the school (approx. 1 mile) and arrived at Belchers Lane Bridge, adjacent to the school, at 8.30am in time to see three trains before going into the school. One was a London express with a 'Jubilee' class usually one of Bushbury's fleet, one a local with a 2-6-4 tank. However the most interesting a semi fast – usually a black five but it could be something more interesting. A Royal Scot, patriot, mogul or one of the new 'standards' could be seen. There was also the occasional freight with a 'super D' or a mogul.

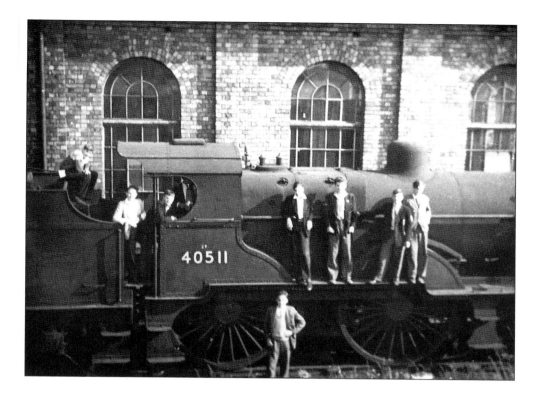

Saltley Grammar School Railway Club on a visit to Bournville shed in 1959 The author is the only one not on the engine.

When it came to sports I was a bit of a non participant – hated rugby and athletics and tried to get out of them. I would tell my mother that I felt unwell or had a pain in my leg. This would prompt a written note asking me to be excused. The PE teacher, Mr Shakespeare, knew I was bluffing but with a parent's note had no option but to excuse me. This meant that while everyone was on the rugby or athletics field I could stand at the edge of the playing field and train spot! Mr Shakespeare had his revenge – I could not be excused from all sport/PE and I recall how he seemed to pick on me and make me do extra press ups etc.!

I formed a loco spotters club whilst at the school and a group of us lads would arrange trips to places of local interest including shed visits. I also produced a little news sheet which recorded lists of locos 'on shed' and interesting or rare visitors to the area. We also dabbled in model railways, the old Hornby Dublo 3 rail, building a small layout in the art room.

Needless to say there were bullies who thought that train spotting was childish or cissy. I often had my school cap flipped off and thrown over the railway fence or my notebook taken and all the numbers scribbled out or the page ripped up. Perseverance won out in the end and the bullies tired of their antics and picked on somebody else.

As mentioned earlier I progressed well at school, so well that I was put into a "fast stream" This meant I was able to take my GCE 'O' levels in four years instead of five, effectively jumping from year two to year four. This meant that my fifth year was for GCE retakes (of which I only had two) and to start 'A' levels.

My interest in railways was at a peak, it was 1959 there was so much to see and do. I struggled with 'A' levels, partly because I was devoting time to my hobbies of railways and football, partly because the late 1950s music scene was exciting. I was captivated; Jerry Lee Lewis, Little Richard, Johnny and the Hurricanes and all the American and British pop artists. Everyone was trying to jump on the bandwagon.

Saltley Grammar School railway club visiting Tyseley shed in 1959. The author is the middle one of the three lads in front of Hall 5988 Bostock Hall. In the background are the shed building and mogul 7318.

In my class two lads, Barry Harber and Colin Tooley, were both learning to play guitar snatching every opportunity between lessons. I tried to play guitar and drums but couldn't get the hang of it. Colin and Barry formed a group and I went to watch them as they progressed from performing in the school, then a local pub and then the Birmingham Town Hall. Colin changed his name to Carl Wayne and formed the Vikings. He then went on to be a member of the Move with several number one hits. After a period of solo work he progressed to be lead singer with the Hollies! Sadly he passed away at the early age of 61 in 2004 – fond memories Colin.

I was probably also a little conceited at having achieved seven GCE passes – all I needed to work on the railways which was my ambition I wanted an apprenticeship at Derby works. I applied and was granted an interview at the recruitment centre in Queens Drive, New Street station. I remember there was a superb model of a Black 5 in the window, I entered, smartly dressed thinking this is the start of my railway career. I was asked a few questions which I answered easily and was then asked to look at some coloured lights and coloured dots in a book. Devastation! I was told I had a red and green colour deficiency which I had never been aware of before. This meant I could not work on the railway and was a massive disappointment and took some coming to terms with.

I was now struggling as to which direction to go in. Stay at school and complete 'A' levels and possibly go into civil engineering or leave school and enter some other profession. This was spring of 1960. A mate of mine Joe had a relative in Gateshead just outside Newcastle. He had been invited to stay there for a week, would I like to go with him? You bet I would, all those steam sheds in North-East England. We could buy a North-East rail rover – visit all the North-East sheds – travel the lines.

I didn't need much persuading, it was on, during school term time as well – naughty, naughty! (More about this trip later). I had told my parents that I was not going to stay on at school – they were upset but they did not try to dissuade me.

I duly went on my Northeast travels and on my return was effectively told by the head teacher that I may as well leave at the end of term! I have had no regrets about my (or was it his!) decision.

I left school and started an engineering apprenticeship at the Morris Commercial Adderley Park in September 1960, more of this later.

Chapter 13

ON YER BIKE!

I always had a bike or a scooter, or so it seems. I can recall a little tricycle which I used to push along with my feet until I got the hang of pedalling. This was superseded by a larger tricycle which I was very proud of – black in colour, front brakes, little footpads at the back for a 'passenger' to stand on.

Traffic was very sparse and cycling along the road was relatively safe. I used to have races with other children – down the Nansen road hill and across Tarry road at the bottom, past the two corner shops. I recall cornering too fast and tipping over with resulting bumps and grazes – also braking too hard and going 'over the top'. It is surprising the injuries I sustained weren't more serious.

The other form of transport was the "go carts" or "mokes" that we made ourselves. This was usually a plank of wood with another piece of wood front and rear at right angles. Attached to these by various methods were the wheels – usually from an old pram or pushchair. The front axle had to be pivoted to allow it to 'steer'. Steering was effected usually by rope or wire attached to the 'axle' or sometimes by using the feet on the 'axle'. This was the basic 'moke' with various luxury additions like a brake, padded seat, orange box bucket seat, lights, bell, decoration and sometimes a passenger seat! The ingenuity used in building a 'better' moke was incredible – I am certain that this sort of activity must have been better child development than sitting in front of a computer!

My third bike was a red Raleigh bicycle purchased from the local second hand shop and lovingly renovated by myself. I called the bike 'Red Dragon' after one of my favourite named trains. It carried me everywhere – locally around Birmingham and further afield to Stourbridge, Kidderminster, Worcester, Wellington, Shrewsbury, Wolverhampton, Banbury, Nuneaton, Tamworth (the field), Lichfield and Rugby.

I can't ever recall having a lock and chain for it – I would just prop it against a wall while I visited a shed – it was always there when I came back!

I recall cycling to Stourbridge – down the infamous Mucklow hill – brakes virtually useless – flying through the traffic lights at the bottom – thank goodness they were on green! The return journey was arduous, back up the hill in a thunderstorm and having to shelter in a partly built house.

The Red Dragon was brilliant – a joy to ride – only three speeds in a Derailleur gear and I kept it immaculate. Its end came, and almost mine when I was turning left at traffic lights with a bus on my right. The bus took

My brother Philip with his newly acquired air-rifle in the tiny backgarden of 12 Mendip Avenue. On the right is my bike the 'Red Dragon' fully equipped for night tours! This would be about 1960.

101

the corner tight and the next thing I knew my bike had been whisked from under me and I was laying on the road. The bike was half under the bus with buckled wheel and bent forks.

The bus company accepted liability and I was asked to purchase a replacement bike and they would pay for it. I purchased from the same shop a five speed derailleur, blue coloured bike – the maker's name I can't even remember. Cycling was never the same – the bike wasn't as good, traffic was increasing, I had more money to travel by coach and train and to eventually buy my own car. I kept this bike for cycling to local places for a few years before eventually selling it on.

Chapter 14

BROMFORD BRIDGE,
THE MONKEY RUN AND GROWLER HILL

Bromford Bridge was and still is where the Birmingham Outer ring road crosses the Birmingham to Derby railway line at Bromford near Erdington. The whole area has now been massively developed with the M6 motorway, Spine Road, Fort Retail Park and a housing estate, all built around the still intact old Bromford Bridge.

At one time Bromford racecourse was to the East of the bridge and a station accessed off the bridge via wooden stairs opened on race days. The massive Stewarts and Lloyds steel tube mill was to the west of the bridge and the Dunlop, Wolsley and Metro Cammell factories were near, all with rail links. The huge Washwood Heath marshalling yards overlooked by the Nechells gasworks were also to the West of the bridge. Needless to say it was a very busy place and popular with "spotters".

There was the added interest of the murky River Tame spanned by a rickety footbridge. The footbridge carried a pedestrian and cycle path approximately half a mile long connecting Bromford Bridge to Common Lane. This path was affectionately known as the "monkey run" (anyone know why?) and was flanked by sidings, factories and a murky oily stream. It was a useful shortcut from where I lived to Bromford Bridge. It was however very spooky in the dark with no lights, the strange sounds from the factories, smoke, steam, the clanking of shunting and rats – big rats!

At the Common Lane end of the monkey run there was a high embankment on top of which there was a railway line. This line ended at a buffer stop precariously positioned at the edge of the embankment. This was known as Growler Hill because diesel shunters (growlers) hauled wagons up the hill before propelling them down into the marshalling yards. The hill was also a superb vantage point for watching trains on the main line and the activities in the yards. It also gave a view into Metro Cammell where

*Photo taken from 'Growler Hill' of Jubilee 45648 'Wemyss' on a Northbound
holiday express 18th August 1962. In the background is Nechells power station.
Note the range of wagons in Washwood Heath sidings.*

the latest rolling stock destined for the London Underground or some
exotic overseas destination could be seen.

Bromford Bridge was the birthplace of the Bromford Locomotive club.
A group of spotters gathered here on a regular basis, friends were made
and the loco club was formed. The club became one of the best known in
the country and organised outings and visits to railway establishments all
over the British Isles. Friendships have lasted and many members are still
in contact with each other to this day.

BR Standard class 5 no. 73054 pilots Jubilee 45656 Cochrane on a holiday relief train at Bromford Bridge station on 18th August 1962. In the right background is Stewarts and Lloyds steelworks and Nechells power station.

A piece of waste ground adjacent to the bridge was the meeting place, football pitch and cricket ground. In later years members would meet at the Bromford pub or the Green Man pub to make plans, have a game of cards over a pint (or two)!

I have many special memories of Bromford Bridge including Beyer-Garratts hauling long trains of wagons out of the sidings, race day specials with a variety of motive power, Crosti Boiler 9F's, 'The Devonian' Jubilee hauled, sometimes with a Compound attached. There was the constant

Caught in the sunlight amidst the gloom of Birmingham New Street station 44666 awaits departure from platform 9 with the 10.00am to Leeds. 26/3/61 Roy Baker.

clamour from the steel mill and the all pervading smells of industry, smoke and steam.

My fondest memory is of the many hours spent playing football, cricket or just chatting while a seemingly endless amount of steam hauled trains passed by. Anoraks? Well maybe, but it was good harmless fun, exercise and socialising. Three ingredients sadly lacking in today's society.

Chapter 15

BROMFORD LOCOMOTIVE CLUB

As mentioned earlier the Bromford Loco club was started by a group of rail enthusiasts. This group met at Bromford Bridge to socialise, play football and cricket and of course to watch trains. The club was very well organised with a committee who arranged trips around the country visiting engine sheds. There were also social events including regular Friday nights at the Green Man or Bromford pub, ten pin bowling and a Christmas social.

The trips were on average fortnightly and usually on a Sunday when most sheds would be full of engines. There were also two/three day trips to Scotland, Devon and Cornwall and Central and South Wales. These involved either overnight travel, sleeping on the coach, or staying in hotels or youth hostels. The trips were by coach and were very popular, often fully booked months in advance. The daytrips left at 6 o'clock, 7 o'clock or 8 o'clock (am) depending on the destination and arrived back late evening. There were several pickup points in Erdington, Bromford and Washwood Heath. My pickup point was the corner of Washwood Road and Herrick Road about 15 minutes walk from home. Members came from a large area including Coventry, Warwick, Kenilworth, Nuneaton and Solihull.

As with any group of people there was a real mix of characters, many with nicknames. Ones I remember are "pongo" (for obvious reasons), "badger" (not sure why), "Dozy" (always sleeping), "Kenilworth Joe", "Western Joe" (worked on the western region of BR), "puke" (always being sick on coach trips), "fudge" (accused of writing down numbers of engines he had not seen), "porky" (always eating porkpies). My own nickname was "nightshirt" (after the dark blue shirt I always wore on trips!)

There are some real tales and incidents associated with these trips. I recall the trip to the North West of England, this was a late Saturday evening departure and included visits to Carnforth, Barrow, Workington and Carlisle. Everything was fine until the coach left Barrow and made its way along the coast road to Workington. It was the middle of the night and people were trying to sleep, the road twisted and turned and went up and

Members of the Bromford Loco. Club at Liverpool Road Halt 13th May 1962.
Author 3rd from left.

down like a rollercoaster. I recall the coach stopping in the middle of nowhere, most of the occupants getting off and either being sick or emptying their bladders against a fence, some doing both at the same time.

Stops could not be made every time someone felt sick or wanted the loo. I remember "puke" always had a supply of brown paper bags, he would vomit into and then throw them out of the window, once I recall in a busy shopping centre! Lemonade bottles were useful as a makeshift loo, and sometimes, very dangerously, someone in desperate need would stand on the step of the coach with the door open and pee into the wind. The coach drivers were generally very tolerant of us and I recall we had two regular drivers who didn't mind our arduous demands and often "laddish" behaviour.

Some of the club members misbehaved and had to be warned by the committee about their behaviour. This included climbing onto engines, removing shed plates or other items from engines. I recall one notorious occasion passing through Merthyr Tydfil when some of these unruly members bared their bums at a congregation leaving the chapel. These members were banned from future club trips after this.

One club member who hailed from Coventry wanted to visit many more sheds particularly those in remote locations. He bought a van and proceeded to cover thousands of miles on a provisional driving licence! The last time I saw him he still hadn't passed his driving test!

BROMFORD LOCO SHED TRIPS

Date	Sheds	Price		Departure
		S. D.	Dec.	
14/6/59	South Wales: 86E/86A/86B/88B/86C/88C/ Radyr/88E/88D/86K/Dowlais/Cae Haris/Rhymney	18 0	£0.90	7am
28/6/59	East Anglia/ Lincolnshire: 34E/31F/Spalding/40F/40A/41K/ 36E/16C/16B/16D	19 0	£0.95	6am
19/6/59	North Wales: 89A/84K/84J/6A/6D/6e/6B/6K/ 6G/6H	20 0	£1.00	7am
16/8/59	Eastern Counties: 34E/31F/31B/31A/30C/30B/ 34C/14C/1E	21 0	£1.05	7am
30/8/59	South Wales: 87A and subsheds/ 87B/87C/87D/87K/87E/ Upper Bank/87F/Burry Port/ 87G	21 0	£1.05	7am
6/9/59	Yorkshire: 50C/50A/53A/53B/53C53E/ 36C/40B	23 0	£1.15	6am
20/9/59	North West: 11A/11B/12A/12B/12C/12D/ Penrith/11D/11C/24L/24J	32 0	£1.60	Midnight
18/10/59	London: 34A/30A/34A/81A/1A/14D/14A/ 14B/1D/33A	17 0	£0.85	6am
5/11/59	Swindon shed and works/82D and subshed/Radstock/82F/82A/ 82B/82E/85B/85E	18 0	£0.90	7am

Chapter 16

ROVING THE RAILS

Many of my train spotting trips were made by coach and later by car but there was no substitute for rail travel. The excitement of it, the feeling of it, the movement, sounds and smells of it – steam, smoke and bitumen unique to railways. The corridors, compartments, toilets, drop down windows, luggage racks, guards vans and the unnerving passage from coach to coach through the narrow bucking connections.

There were always good deals to be had in rail travel and it was convenient, flexible and easy to use. There was a wide range of cheap fares available including rail rover tickets in a variety of forms. There was one which gave freedom to travel the entire rail network in England, Scotland and Wales for seven or fourteen days. There were regional ones – Western, Southern, Scottish etc. and there were area ones – in particular 'holiday runabout tickets'.

They were great value and I took advantage of this when on holiday with my parents. I also regularly purchased a Midland runabout ticket giving travel between Shrewsbury, Matlock, Trentham, Malvern, Nuneaton, Stratford, and Leamington for one week for £1.75! (1960). All one needed was a BR timetable, a little preparation time and stamina!

In June 1960 I had a friend 'Joe' who had relatives in Gateshead, Newcastle on Tyne. He arranged for us to stay with the relatives for a week and we would have a rover ticket. I was still at school but decided it was a great opportunity, too good to miss. So I truanted from school and off we went.

We travelled by train to Newcastle and caught the bus to Gateshead, finding ourselves in a run down area with rows of terraced houses, many in course of demolition. The house was small but cosy and friendly – outside loo, no bathroom and coal fires, just like home really. However it was a good base for our week's spotting.

Joe's relatives were friendly if somewhat bemused by our exploits. In the evening they would take us to a nearby working men's club where we were made welcome by the local 'Geordies'.

It was a brilliant week – we covered every inch of track on the rover ticket including trips to Middleton in Teesdale and Towlaw – both DMUs unfortunately.

We also went to Carlisle, the branch to Alston, the 'loop' around north Tyneside and visited the sheds of South Blyth, North Blyth, Percy Main, Heaton and managed to spend some time at Whitley Bay on the beach!

We would catch the bus into Newcastle passing the redundant shed at Borough Gardens. Then to the magnificent Central station where we would catch our train to whichever destination we were bound. The bridges over the Tyne fascinated me and we crossed each one of them during the week by road, rail or on foot!

During the week we visited the sheds at Blaydon, Carlisle Kingmoor and Canal, Gateshead, Sunderland, West Hartlepool, Thornaby, Darlington, West Auckland, North and South Blyth, Percy Main and Tyne dock. We had no permits and we were fortunate to bunk the sheds or get permission with no problems. However the real highlights were: the run down the coast behind A1 "Straight Deal" passing the Staithes at Seaham and the docks at Hartlepool. Then into Stockton with its curved station roof and the

Newcastle Central Station with A3 60086 Sir Hugo about to leave south bound. In the background is type 4 diesel D276. 5th July 1960. I should have been in school!

North British Reid design 'Glen' 4-4-0 62488 Glen Aladale at Carlisle Citadel 5th July 1960.

surrounding chemical works with its 'plumb crazy' pipework. Onto Darlington with its impressive station building, old engine "Locomotion" on the platform and the roar of through expresses roving past behind the canopy – unable to see the numbers!

Then the wonderful ride up the valley to Middleton in Teesdale. It was a DMU but gave the advantage of offering a driver's eye view as the magnificent scenery opened up. The DMU only stopped in Middleton for 10 minutes before returning and as the next was a couple of hours later we didn't stick around. In hindsight I wish we had taken time to have a look round. We changed at Barnard Castle – another station with an overall roof – for the trip to Bishop Auckland and Tow Law. The return was to Sunderland via Durham.

We travelled the lines covered by the roundabout ticket several times during the week but also went further a field. The highlight was a trip behind a B1 to Carlisle, seeing a 'Glen' at Citadel station and the branch from Haltwhistle to Alston (another DMU). We also visited Blaydon shed – expecting to hear a chorus of 'Blaydon Races' but were disappointed.

A great week – many hundreds of miles of rail travel mainly by steam, lots of 'cops' and wonderful Geordie hospitality.

When I got home and returned to school the head teacher suggested that as my heart was not really in studying for 'A' levels perhaps I should leave school!

A few weeks later I was roving the rails again! This time it was at the opposite end of the country on the south coast. My parents, brother and sister and I went on holiday to Weymouth staying in a caravan at Chesil Beach camp near Portland.

We travelled by coach this time – a great disappointment – but I had already worked out my schedule for the week. My parents were used to me by now and accepted that I would be a 'lodger' at the caravan and may spend some time with them during the week in between spotting!

I purchased an area 10 holiday roundabout ticket which gave me freedom of the lines from Weymouth to Brockenhurst and Lymington including Bournemouth, Swanage branch and the New Forest line through Ringwood. I travelled all the lines including the Weymouth Quay line and once again paid excess fares to Salisbury, Eastleigh and Southampton to visit the sheds and works.

I also caught the ferry from Lymington Pier to Yarmouth Isle of Wight and travelled the Isle of Wight network – Yarmouth to Newport, Ryde and Sandown/Ventnor. I visited the shed and works at Ryde – seeing all the Isle of Wight locos! I was the envy of my mates when I got home!

During the week I had some fabulous journeys behind a wide range of locos including Pacifics, 34017 "Ilfracombe", 34058 "Sir Frederick Pile", 34095 "Mortehoe" and 34093 "Saunton", 35027 "Portline" and 35020 "Bibbyline". I also travelled behind 76019, 30796, 92206 (Poole to Salisbury), 73082, 30107, 30790, 75073, 75077, 73084, 4945 and "Isle of Wight" locos 22, 20 and 4. Highlights of the week were watching standard class 5's banking heavy trains up Broadway Bank out of Weymouth, School class 30910 Merchant Taylor at Yeovil Junction, the Isle of Wight, the trip through Weymouth to the docks.

Notes I made in my notebook include "Rolling stock fly shunted into Weymouth station and slowed down using rail retarders" "loco 1369 on Weymouth docks line encountered deep flood water from a burst pipe – attempted to go through but got stuck. Fire engine had to rescue!" "Buses from Chesil beach caravan site to Weymouth leave at 6.50am, 7.04, 7.14, 7.31". I bet my parents were pleased!

My parents enjoyed a drink in the local pub near Chesil Beach in the evenings and I joined them one evening – very sociable of me!

Local fishermen used the pub and would sell off some of their catch. My father who loved fish (catching and eating) bought a huge flat fish which I carried back to the caravan. It lasted for a couple of meals before it was eventually thrown to the seagulls.

Riding the rails locally was made easy by purchasing a Midland or Town holiday runabout ticket.

I loved these – they gave freedom to travel around a wide area of the Midlands and by paying a reasonable excess fare many other interesting places could be reached. The other bonus of course was that you were 'homebased' with the associated comforts. I would prepare in advance working out a 'timetable' for the week including the excess 'bits'.

I have a detailed record of a week in July 1963 using a runabout ticket to its full advantage as follows:

14th July New Street-Derby (pulled by black five 44856)
Derby-Matlock DMU
Matlock-Buxton DMU
Visit Buxton MPD
Buxton-Stockport
Visit Stockport MPD
Stockport-Manchester
Visit Trafford Park and Newton Heath MPD's
Return to Birmingham (pulled by Derby-Birmingham 44806)

15th July Snow Hill-Wolverhampton (D1109)
Wolverhampton-Wellington (6996)
Wellington-Stafford (45572)
Visit Stafford MPD
Stafford-Nuneaton (D222)
Nuneaton-New Street (75052)

16th July Snow Hill-Chester via Shrewsbury
Visit Chester MPD
Chester-Bangor
Visit Bangor MPD
Bangor-Holyhead
Visit Holyhead MPD
Holyhead-Birmingham via Chester and Shrewsbury

17th July New Street-Burton on Trent
Visit Burton MPD
Burton-Derby (45668)
Derby-New Street (73170)

18th July New Street-Derby (45674)
Derby Friar Gate-Nottingham Victoria
Visit Colwick MPD
Nottingham Victoria-Derby Friar Gate
Derby Midland-Rowsley
Visit Rowsley MPD
Rowsley-Derby (75041)
Derby-New Street (61225)

19th July Snow Hill-Shrewsbury (7918)
Shrewsbury-Oswestry
Visit Oswestry MPD
Oswestry-Snow Hill via Shrewsbury (1014 County of Glamorgan)
New Street-Worcester Shrub Hill (73092)
Worcester Shrub Hill-Worcester Foregate (4628)
Visit Worcester MPD
Worcester-Snow Hill (6879)

BRANCH LINE WANDERINGS

I have already mentioned the thrill of riding the rails – often it was the excitement of speed behind a 'King' or a 'Royal Scot'. There was also the quaintness of a meandering journey along a rural line to a quiet country town. I wished I had done more (don't we all) before they fell to the 'Beeching Axe' but I do remember the following journeys:

Worcester to Bromyard behind a Pannier no. 4614. The line which continued onto Leominster was closed and overgrown with weeds. I recall passing through orchards and hopfields to the small station where the engine ran round. I think there were about six passengers on a two coach train.

LLANYMYNECH TO LLANFYLLIN

The train started at Oswestry and ran up this little branch behind 46512. The only memory I have of this is the comment from a bemused guard who wondered why we had got off the train and got straight back on again.

115

WORCESTER TO SHREWSBURY – THE SEVERN VALLEY

I was really pleased that I travelled this line in the days of steam. The loco was 82007 and went via Hartlebury, Stourport, Bewdley and Bridgnorth. I recall passing the Ironbridge, the power station at Buildwas and the strange station there with upper and lower platforms. This is where the Wellington to Much Wenlock branch crossed – another line I travelled. In this area I also did Wellington to Stafford and Wellington to Crewe via Market Drayton.

REDDITCH TO TEWKESBURY

The line from Redditch to Tewkesbury went via Evesham and Ashchurch. Tewkesbury amazed me with its tiny engine shed housing 3 locos including BR standard 75023.

I then continued to Gloucester and onto Hereford via Ross on Wye returning via Worcester.

Oxford to Fairford via Witney I managed to travel the long, long branch from Oxford to Fairford via Witney – the loco was Pannier 9789 and the journey was a round trip of 50 miles.

Branch line wanderings. I travelled to Tewkesbury from Birmingham via Redditch and Evesham. Pannier 4614 is almost ready to return to Evesham from Ashchurch. 1st June 1962.

LOCAL BRANCHES

Closer to home I travelled the lines from Wolverhampton to Stourbridge via Himley. Stourbridge-Walsall via Dudley and Walsall-Lichfield via Brownhills.

There was still a service from Birmingham to Walsall via Sutton Park through Walmley and Streetly which I did behind Push-Pull Ivatt 41224.

Chapter 17

THE KNITTING MACHINE LADY
(AND HER SON)

I can't remember how I got to know Ken but he and I became close friends with a shared interest in railways. I think we met at Saltley Grammar school and became good enough friends for me to be invited to his house about half a mile from where I lived. He was an only child and a bit of a loner – I think his parents were pleased that he had made a friend.

Visits to his house had several attractions. Firstly his mom always served up pop and cakes! Secondly he had an '0' gauge rail electric train set with lots of track, points, signals, stations and several locos – some with headlights.

One was a Princess Royal class, another was a large American style loco, probably worth a lot now. We would spend hours laying out track with loops and sidings on the carpeted floor (my house only had linoleum!)

Another attraction was that they had a television! My parents must have been the last people in Birmingham to have a television and I was captivated by it watching classics like the Lone Ranger, Ivanhoe and Robin Hood.

There was one slight downside to visiting Ken's and that was the dog. They had a very old, very large, brown and white dog who slobbered everywhere and created the most awful smells. Everyone laughed at it and I suffered it for the cakes, model railway and TV.

However there was another major benefit of knowing Ken – his mother, a very large, jovial person, was a sales demonstrator for a knitting machine company. She had a company van and would go around demonstrating the machine to potential customers. During the school holidays she would take Ken and myself out with her and drop us off at some convenient 'spotting' venue and pick us up later in the day. She would provide a bag of food and drink and off we would go. There was no radio in the van and she would entertain us singing songs of the day and children's favourites. I remember frequent renditions of 'Nellie the elephant', 'Thumbelina', 'Ugly Duckling' and 'You're a pink toothbrush' plus many others.

She often made visits to Derbyshire and Nottinghamshire and would leave us at Ambergate with its triangular station, Bottesford, Grantham, Loughborough and Newark. Ken would sit in the passenger seat beside his mom and I would sit on a cushion in the back beside the knitting machines! When I left school we went our separate ways and I lost contact with Ken but I have some great memories of him and his mom, the 'Knitting Machine Lady'.

Chapter 18

NO MONEY – NO TRIPS!

Throughout this book there are descriptions of many train spotting trips all over the country. Some were by train, some by coach and later by car. Some involved overnight stays and associated costs.

Even outings in the early years to local places often involved bus fares and train fares. On top of this was the cost of notebooks, pens, pencils, Ian Allan ABC's and shed directories. Expensive hobby was train spotting!

So where did the money come from? Bearing in mind that my peak spotting time was from the age of nine until about twenty two.

In 1952 when I started, food rationing was still in force, money was tight and there was little to spare for luxuries. I don't recall having pocket money but do remember running errands for neighbours and receiving a few coppers.

As my spotting in those days was all local, walking distance or a bus ride (with my parents), costs were minimal. All I needed was paper and pencil and I saved my pennies for events to come. As I grew older I had more freedom to move further afield and was given some pocket money but also increased my errand running. One that bought in a fair amount was coke collecting from the gasworks. This involved collecting a wheeled container – old wheelbarrow or pram from a neighbour, going to the gasworks and waiting in a long queue for a half or whole hundredweight of coke. Then it had to be pushed up Alum Rock Road (a steepish hill) and back to the neighbours. Rewards were good for this service and I started accumulating money in my Municipal Bank account.

I was now able to pay for trips to Tamworth, Lichfield and Worcester. Then came the real breakthrough into high finance – a paper round! I think I was 12 when I started my first paper round at Foley's newsagent on the corner of Gowan Road and Alum Rock Road, opposite the Rock Public house. I loved it – the camaraderie of the other lads, reading the comics on the way round, the occasional tip. Except on Sundays – just like today,

Sunday papers were bulky and heavy. A double delivery was needed to get them all out – luckily there were no Sunday evening papers!

The owner of the shop, Mrs Foley, was an elderly lady who often went away – she said she had malaria and had to go into hospital for treatment. When she was off she would leave a lad in charge – he was older than me. He was a bully and would make our lives a misery. However, he had his comeuppance when it was found he was stealing from the shop – I remember the police coming in one day when Mrs Foley was in the shop. We were asked questions about the 'bully' – but he never returned.

I must have impressed Mrs Foley as she asked if I would cover the shop for her mornings and evenings. She would come in during the day when I was at school. This was great and I soon learned the ropes and was able to manage the shop single handed. The downside was having to be at the shop at 5.30 am to take delivery of the morning papers – then there would be customers at 6.00 am! She gave me keys to lock and unlock and allowed me to run the shop at weekends when I could. All this gave a massive boost to my income and funded my many trips around the country.

My first visit to London included Hornsey shed with its large stud of J50's 12/6/60.

There was an extra earner and this was selling the Sports Argus on Saturday evening under a lamppost opposite the shop. Cars would stop, people would come out and I would get through two to three hundred copies! However it was an outdoor job and I would be out there on all weathers – including a heavy snowfall when I must have looked like the abominable snowman! I recall at one time the Argus was 3d and I got 1d for each one sold – that's £2/£3 profit, a lot of money in the 1950s!

In fact when I started work in 1960 as an apprentice at Morris Commercial, my weekly pay was nineteen shillings – less than my Sports Argus takings! I did continue with my newsagent shop work after I started full time work and it was a useful top up to my miserable wage.

Chapter 19

THE NUMBERS GAME

Spotting engine numbers (and names) was all about trying to see as many as possible and record them in the ABC books. The best way to do this was by 'shed bashing' visiting a large number of sheds usually on a Sunday when they were full.

I have some examples of this which may be of interest to readers and certainly provide an interesting insight into the range of locos operating.

27TH SEPTEMBER 1959
Stephenson Locomotive Society Golden Jubilee Visit to Derby and Nottingham with Midland Compound no. 1000.

This was special – Compound no. 1000 beautifully turned out in Midland Red (although mechanically not too good!) Crowds of people everywhere along the route, "whistle blown at every station, blokes on the bank, old ladies, old men, girls and boys cheering and waving", I wrote in my notebook.

Numbers written down as follows:

New Street 45353, 1000.

Saltley (passing) 48733, 48718, 40180, 46492, 44747, 44943, 45058, 58138, 44263, 43709, 40457, 43347, 58165, 44315.

Water Orton 58315, 43709, 40453, 43327, 58305, 58128, 42756.

Burton on Trent, 40675, 42308, 58157, 40452, 40553, 41083, 41122,

Derby 41113, 58225, 43300, 58151, 40567, 58130,

Derby Works 42184, 73043, 46499, 58158, 47563, 44142, 10201, 10202, D3091, D30308, D3790, D3791, D3792, D3788, 11126, 12036, D2, D5, D6, D7, D8, D9, 48552, D5023, 10100, 12082, 12000, 40037, 44267, 47681, D3787, D5024, 44327, D5066/67/68/69/70. 44122, 47428, 44169, 48274, 75046, 48108, 48672, 42515, 42514, 80040, 48177, 42686, 42227, 44187, 42311, 43496, 43935, 48274, 48600, 48687, 80091, 42624, D5025/26/27/28, D5709, 48107, 48293, 73030, 43979, 80091, 10800, 47309, 40680, 42354, 58191, 40332, 43886, 58217, 42422, 42184, 48390,

D3172, 12034, D3074, D3785/86, 44540, 12072, D5700/01/04/07/12/14/15, 40925, 43435.

Derby Shed 41773, 73139, 44851, 43200, 47660, D3776, D3570/76/ 85/86, 73144, 43306, 45626, 43991, 42053, 44601, 73157, 43735, 45279, 48510, 48121, 44545, 42054, 44164, 73158, 41157, 46103, 46502, 45656, 73136, 48466, 92122, 46500, 44943, 73142, 44688, 44981, 46443, 45278, 42140, 44139, 42760, D5702/08/10/11/13/, 41121, 43957, 43553, 47413, 47429, 44402, 46133, 42822, 45608, 46497, 43658, 42896, 42517, D1, 44465, 45610, D3, 42346, D3773, 47386, 44560, 12033, 48715, 48764, 90012, 43243, 42281, 42353, 44304, 42257, 41847, 44539, 43548, 44389, 48313, 44214, 44335, 44355, 42184, 80093, 47205, 44529, 44500, 43840, 43368, 44419, 43459, 43325, 44098, 44048, 44472, 48346, 44334, 44154, 90282, 44278, 48079, 44458, 48507, 48270, 46402, 46440, 58219, 58144, 43771, 43274, 43186, 58192, 47249, 43727, 43731, 43222, 43183, 42308, 40675, 41763, 45407.

Toton Shed 48370, 44224, 44376, 48603, 48363, 48685, 44229, 45137, 48033, 43921, 48607, 48384, 43826, 44106, 48446, 48750, 48657, 48196, 48187, D3121, 42617, 48118, 92050, 92112, 92131, 45116, 43031, 48127, 48362, 48690, 48314, 92158, 92130, 48651, 92123, 48271, 42763, 48197, 48221, D3582, D3117, D3122, 43845, 12055, 48338, D3118/19/20/23, 44012, D3576, D3126, 43309, 92077, 48332, 48414, 43832, D3124,/25, 12038, 92156, 48338, 48119, 48125, 41947, 48088, 47551, 48319, 48545, 44200, 48062, 42783, 48124, 48637, 48380, 92153, 49145, 43860, 44088, 43865, 44410, 44140, 44161, 43990, 58153/66/73, 43650, 43499, 48407, 48060, 48132, 44176, 48303, 48606, 43453, 44129, 48109, 48440, 43235, 44170, 43793, 48194, 48615, D10.

Nottingham Shed 40513, 44853, 44182, 40175, 44550, 42769, 48201, 44313, 48635, 48261, 43507, 48000, 75056, 48170, 43958, 44394, 44585, 40682, 43954, 43856, 44418, 44158, 48279, 43962, 43918, 40585, 43070, 44031, 48765, 48454, 48377, 44132, 48416, 48217, 44033, 44195, 43995, 48666, 44248, 48696, 48513, 48639, 48653, 42931, 44983, 42185, 45088, 40454, 45333, 75062, 42161, 75063, 44658, 42636, 40411, 45263, 75064, 40504, 44804, 44944, 45641, 12050, 92012, 12097, 12098, D3083/85, D3246/47, D3290, 12051/52, D3084, 45667, 48215, 43251, 48214, 44546, 47277, 44480, 44204, 47631, 44095, 44021, 44412, 44555, 44018, 58175, 61440, 44190, 70015, 44131, 48617, 48391, 48007, 48728.

During the Whitsun holiday May 20th, 21st/22nd 1961 I went on a "shed bashing" tour of Scotland as follows:

SATURDAY 20TH MAY

12C Carlisle Canal (4.24 am!) 29 steam, 12A Carlisle Kingmoor (5.05 am!) 87 steam, 7 diesel. 64G Hawick (6.35 am!) 10 steam, Galashiels 3 steam 1 diesel, 64A St. Margaret's Edinburgh (9.00 am) 61 steam, 13 diesel, Seafield 7 steam, Southleith 2 steam, 5 diesel, 64C Dalry Road 12 steam, 1 diesel, 64B Haymarket 22 steam, 8 diesel, 64F Bathgate 22 steam, 2 diesel, 65K Polmont 20 steam, 1 diesel, 65F Grangemouth 23 steam, 2 diesel, Bowness 26 steam, Forfar 14 steam, Aberdeen station 4 steam, 3 diesel.

Sunday 21st May 61B Aberdeen Ferry Hill 31 steam 18 diesel, 61A Kitty Brewster 21 steam, 23 diesel, Montrose 2 steam, 62B Dundee 37 steam, 9 diesel, 63A Perth 62 steam, 15 diesel, 62A Thornton 56 steam, 5 diesel. 62C Dunfermline 33 steam, 5 diesel, Alloa 6 steam, 3 diesel, 65J Stirling 23 steam, 8 diesel, 65E Kipps 41 steam, 11 diesel, 66B Motherwell 97 steam, 14 diesel, 66C Hamilton 18 steam, 66A Polmadie (Glasgow) 114 steam, 23 diesel.

Monday 22nd May 65C Parkhead 44 steam, 7 diesel, 65B St. Rollox 44 steam, 21 diesel, 65A Eastfield Glasgow 64 steam, 34 diesel, 65D Dawsholm 42 steam, 5 diesel, Glasgow Central Station 12 steam, 1 diesel, 67A Corker Hill 47 steam, 6 diesel, 66 D Greenock 18 steam, 2 diesel, 67D Ardrossan 33 steam, 1 diesel, 67B Hurlford 42 steam, 2 diesel. 67C Ayr 30 steam, 68B Dumfries 32 steam, 12A Carlisle Kingmoor 90 steam, 6 diesel, 12B Carlisle Upperby 64 steam, 4 diesel.

The most locomotives I spotted in one day was on a tour of London sheds in 1959 with 1052 numbers written down! Approx 5% of the total operating in Britain!

Chapter 20

LOCOMOTIVE SHEDS

During the course of my spotting years I travelled the length and breadth of Britain by train, coach, car, bike and ferry in pursuit of engines. Engine sheds were the places to go to see a number of engines in a short space of time especially on a Sunday. In 1960 there were over 500 sheds and I visited all but 20 of them!

Engine sheds came in all different sizes, types, shapes and locations. Some were 'straight' with parallel lines or 'roads' of engines, others had 'roundhouses' with a central turntable and engine 'roads' radiating out from it. Some of the bigger sheds had a mixture of both. Many were in the middle of a heavily industrialised area and others were in idyllic country or seaside locations. The smallest shed I visited was Clee Hill in Shropshire with one small tank loco, this was a sub shed of Shrewsbury. The largest was Stratford in London covering a large area and containing 225 locos on my visit in 1959.

The legal way to visit a shed was to obtain a permit from a regional office, the illegal way was to find a way in without being seen and hope not to get caught. This was known as 'bunking' a shed. The third way was to politely ask the shed foreman if he would allow a visit, of course if he said no it made bunking more difficult!

My favourite sheds were those in the South Wales valleys, places like Aberbeeg, Aberdare, Treherbet, Abercynon, Rhymney and Ferndale. Arriving by road the sheds could be seen nestling in the valley surrounded by hills, pitheads, coalwagons, slag heaps and rows of miners terraced houses.

Then there were the 'giants' in London – the Cathedral like Old Oak Common with its four roundhouses, Kings and Castles, polished brass and Nine Elms surrounded by tower blocks. There was Kings Cross with its fleet of Pacifics including the A4 streaks, Willesden with its huge allocation of mainly freight engines and, as mentioned earlier, sprawling Stratford.

In winter sheds could be gruesome places. I remember Annesley in the snow, coal had been stockpiled some 20ft high and we had to clamber over this, slippery and dirty to reach a line of stored locos. Blackpool and Fleetwood in a blizzard, not many people on the beach! Lower Darwen on top of a hill near Blackburn, gale force winds and driving sleet. I remember going to Consett in the North East in mid winter. The coach (there was no access by train) had to plough through snow drifts. Consett was a small village high up and only there for the steel works.

There were remote outposts, none more so than the sheds on the Cromford and High Peak line in Derbyshire. I recall walking up a cable incline from Cromford village to reach the little shed at Middleton where one of Rowsley sheds J94 0-6-0 tanks was stabled.

One of the most impressive sheds was at Thornaby, newly built in the 60s to replace the ancient sheds at Stockton an Middlesborough. Spacious and clean it must have been pleasant for the enginemen.

The atmosphere in sheds varied greatly. The large sheds were always a hive of noise and activity, locos being prepared for duty, watered, coaled, oiled and greased. Smoke and steam, dust and spray, large coaling towers active and noisy. There were locos being cleaned after duty, ash shovelled from smokeboxes, red hot embers and clinker, the sighing of steam being emptied. Loco's being turned and shunted, wheezing, clanking, sizzling, snuffling. On the floor hazardous piles of hot ash, oily pools of water, sand and soot, bricks and brakes. Some sheds were untidy and there were other hazards like fireirons, firebars, rags, buckets and cans to be negotiated. Interiors of sheds were generally poorly lit, murky, smoky. There were the shed staff, drivers, firemen, cleaners, maintenance, checking their turn of duty and their allocated locomotives.

Smaller sheds were on the whole cleaner and less hazardous and on Sundays would be shut down completely with just a hiss a sizzle or a drip from an engine as if to say 'I'm still alive'.

Chapter 21

DUCKS, CRABS AND FLYING PIGS

This book is about railways, trainspotting and life in the fifties and sixties, so where do animals, birds and crustaceans come into it?

Well, it's all to do with nicknames. Many locomotives, steam, diesel and electric were given names according to their appearance, size, sound, motion or other peculiarity.

'Ducks' was the name given to the Fowler 4F Midland 0-6-0 tender engines 43835 to 44606, the larger Fowler 0-8-0 engines 49500 to 49674 were often called 'Duck eights'. The engines waddled from side to side when moving in a duck like fashion, however the name probably originates from the '0' wheel arrangement – 'Duck' being a term in cricket for no runs (0) being scored.

'Crabs' were the Hughes Mogul 2-6-0 engines numbered 42700 to 42944. They had inclined cylinders and a raised running board over the cylinders. When in motion the inclined cylinders caused the engine to rock from side to side in a crabbing motion.

'Flying Pigs' were the Ivatt 2-6-0 moguls 43000-43161. They had very high running boards for ease of maintenance which looked like small wings. They were generally considered unattractive in appearance, hence 'pigs' The two features combined gave the 'flying pigs' nickname. They were also called 'doodlebugs 'although I don't know why.

The Ivatt 2-6-2 tank engines 41200 to 41329 were called 'Mickey Mouses'. This may have been to their twee tininess or to their 'Mikado' wheel arrangement.

The diminutive 0-4-0 saddle tank engines 51200 to 51253 were known as 'pugs', presumably because of their size, snub nose and snapping around the shunting yards!

Ex. War department locos 90001 to 90731 were called 'dubb dees' a distortion of WD.

One highly unusual name was that given to the unrebuilt Bulleid Pacifics of the West Country and Battle of Britain classes. They were known as 'spam cans', presumably after their shape similar to a can of that well known pork product Spam. It may be in part due to their wartime design although they were not built until after the war (1945 onwards).

Many steam locomotives had smoke deflectors usually attached to the smokebox sides. They were to divert air to push smoke from the chimney upwards to ensure that the driver had clear vision. They looked like the eye shields or 'blinkers' used on horses, the name stuck and could be heard called out by trainspotters 'it's a blinker'! Any tank engine with the tanks 'hanging' from the boiler sides were called pannier tanks for obvious reasons. Tank engines with the tank straddling the boiler were called saddle tanks, again for obvious reasons.

One strange name is 'Duke Dog' given to the Great Western 4-4-0 engines 9000 to 9028. They were in fact rebuilds of previous engines of the Bulldog class and the Duke of Cornwall class, using parts from each class, hence the name.

Modern traction has had its share of nicknames as follows:

Class 08 shunters	Growlers or Gronks	Due to noise made
Class 20	Choppers	Engine noise
Class 24/25	Rats	Rattletraps
Class 40	Whistlers	Noise made
Class 37	Growlers or tractors	Noise made
Class 50	Hoovers	Noise made
Class 45	Peaks	Named after peaks
Class 56	Grid	Noise and fan covers
Class 26 electric	Tommys	Name given to first of class by Dutch
GWR railcars	Flying banana	Shape and colour scheme
Class 43 HST	As above	

To a modern traction enthusiast steam engines are known as 'kettles', conversely steam enthusiasts call diesels 'boxes' and electrics 'sparkies'.

Chapter 22

WORKING LIFE AND
OTHER DISTRACTIONS

The 'swinging 60s?' Certainly the decade bustled with activity and events, some good, some bad.

Firstly I started work in September 1960 at Morris Commercial Cars, Adderley Park as an engineering apprentice. I was at the height of my train spotting – covering the country most weekends, especially Sundays, mainly on trips with the Bromford Loco Society.

However at the age of seventeen there were plenty of other things to grab my attention. I had a great group of 'spotting' friends and we graduated to drinking, ten pin bowling, football, pop music and of course, girls.

I also made new friends with my fellow apprentices and after the 'induction' soon became part of the establishment. The induction was all the usual pranks played on a naïve, unsuspecting lad. I was sent to the stores for a 'long wait', a left handed screwdriver, a new bubble for the spirit level, all joyfully 'dispensed' by the compliant store man.

The apprentice training room was on the third floor overlooking the Birmingham-London line and sidings at Adderley Park. I took every opportunity to 'spot' trains and watched the shunting movements in the yard.

At the far end of the apprentice training room was another room full of typewriters for training office staff. Every afternoon the trainee girls would have to pass through the apprentice room – can you imagine the effect on us hot blooded lads! I think it was deliberate on behalf of management to test our self control!

Music was important, the early 60s saw The Beatles, The Hollies, Rolling Stones and a multitude of other pop groups emerging with exciting sounds. The Brum sound was also important – The Move, Spencer Davis, Moody Blues, Avengers, Redcaps, Fortunes and Mike Sheridan and The Nightriders. We lads would go to pubs and clubs to see these groups, drink and try to meet a member of the opposite sex. Life was pretty good – a good job (albeit with low pay), good friends, music, drink, girls and steam trains!

My parents still lived in the two up, two down terraced house in Alum Rock and as myself, brother and sister became older, space was at a premium? My brother was also very unwell with frequent hospital visits and one of the downs of the 60s was he tragically died at the age of 14 in 1962. This had a devastating effect on the family and I found it very hard to come to terms with.

I was able in 1963 to afford my first car, a 1953 split screen side valve Morris Minor (LFD 573) which cost me £75! This opened up greater opportunities for spotting and that little car covered a few thousand miles. My mates had also bought cars – I remember an old Ford Anglia, an A40 Devon, a Hillman Minx and a Triumph Herald.

We would take it in turns to use our cars to travel around the country. My little Moggy was reliable and I kept it for twelve months before graduating to the luxury of a 1956 Austin A50 Cambridge (OUS 178) which cost me £90. This was followed by another A50 – black with a

BR Standard tank 80138 at Swansea East Dock shed 24th March 1963.

sunshine roof – SOL 177! (funny how I can recall the registration numbers of my old cars but have difficulty in remembering the present one!)

I received excellent engineering training at MCC and spent time in all the departments – production, design, tool room, laboratory, machine shops, repair and maintenance and development. Development is where I chose to make my career – testing vehicles and problem solving appealed – especially as it meant being out and about. However I was sent by my employer to college at Cranfield near Bedford for two years from 1964 to 1966, I then met my future wife in 1965. This coupled with the fact that I had just about spotted every steam locomotive in Britain, generally curtailed my intensive 'spotting' activities.

Chapter 23

THE END (OR IS IT?)

There hasn't really been an ending because even when steam on BR finished in 1968 my enthusiasm for railways continued.

I carried on 'spotting' diesels and electrics but not with the same dedication. I certainly did not make special trips, it was more a case of being near to a railway or a depot (shed) and 'paying a visit' while passing.

My spotting in the days of steam slowed down in 1966 for three reasons. Firstly I had just about spotted every locomotive in the Ian Allan book. Out of approximately 17,000 locos there were only 47 I hadn't seen! These were generally in far flung places which would have involved substantial travel and time with no guarantee of seeing the loco concerned. Secondly girls, young ladies, were diverting my attention away from railways. In 1965 I met the young lady who was to become my wife in 1968. Thirdly, my employer sent me on a two year course full time at a college in Bedford.

I did try to see steam whenever and wherever I could and regret not making more efforts to witness the last days, particularly in the North West.

I do remember the last working steam engine I saw locally – it was 2-8-0 Consol lumbering through Bromford Bridge on a long freight. I was on an outer circle bus and as the bus passed over the bridge, the 8F was on the down slow line. I could not read the number but its memory is still with me. This was in 1966.

Some of the last steam I saw working was at Clapham Junction with standard 2-6-2 tanks – 82019 and 82025 shunting carriages. This was also in 1966, when I had a few days holiday in London.

After this it was the odd day trip or holiday when I caught sight of a steam engine – Blackpool, Southport, Llandudno, Leeds. What was increasingly evident was the lines of "dead" steam engines at various locations awaiting their fate. This filled me with great sadness.

My saviour has been the preserved railway movement and in particular the Severn Valley Railway. I started working voluntarily on the SVR in 1969 and have now realized my boyhood ambition to work on a railway. I have experienced the joy and satisfaction of being a member of a team of enthusiasts who have kept alive the traditions of steam railways. Not just the steam engines but all the artifacts, atmosphere and working customs that go with it.

Imagine a warm sunny day, birds singing, sheep bleating, otherwise peaceful and serene. A quiet country railway station, the Great Western Railway architecture, milk churns, gas lamps and carefully attended flower beds. The smell of freshly polished brass, warm bitumen, floor polish and disinfectant! Waiting passengers chatting idly, the clunk of tickets being date stamped in the booking office. A sudden "ting" from the signal box followed by several other "tings" disturbs the peace. The sound of levers being pulled, the clunk of points changing, the clank of a signal arm being lowered. The faraway whistle of a steam engine, the sound of an engine working, the "clickety clack" of carriage wheels echoing along the line.

The passengers move in anticipation of the arrival, station staff position themselves to receive the train. Now it's closer, hear it breathing, see the smoke and steam, feel the ground trembling. Here it is – 7802 "Bradley Manor" – green paintwork sparkling, brass shining, whisps of steam, hauling a rake of GWR chocolate and cream coaches. The fireman reaches to collect the single line token off the signal man and the driver brings the train to a halt. Feel the warmth from the engine, smell the steam, smoke, oil and coal. Hear the sound of steam, the roar of the blower, the sound of shovel on coal, coach doors slamming.

Then it's a raised arm, a green flag, a "rightaway", a whistle and off. The magnificent sight and sound of a steam engine starting a train, the sharp staccato blast from the chimney, the movement of piston rods, connecting, rods and valve gear. Then it's gone, a distant sound receding. Peace, tranquillity, birds, sheep and a lingering aroma of steam. All these sense and feelings describe a branch line in the 1950s – but this is Arley station, Severn Valley Railway 2006! The end? No, and it never will be.

Chapter 24

THE ONES THAT GOT AWAY!

My ambition was to "spot" every steam engine in England, Scotland and Wales. In 1960 this numbered over 17000 and by the time my "spotting" effectively finished in 1966 I had them all bar 47! The 47 that got away are listed below with their allocations in 1965:

Western Region:
Collett 0-4-2 tank, 1466 (83B Taunton), Panniers 1664 (82C Swindon), 3796 (87F Llanelli), 4610, 4616 (72A Exmouth Junction), 9605 (82C Swindon), Hall 4-6-0 4920 (83D Plymouth Laira), 6935 (86A Newport), Grange 4-6-0 6825 (81D Reading), 6873 (82B Bristol St. Philip's Marsh), 2-8-0 tank 5220 (88L Cardiff).

Southern Region:
2-6-0 30827, 30829, 30842 (72A Exmouth Junction), 31793 (71A Eastleigh), 31834 (72A Exmouth Junction), 34011, 34023, 34079 (72A Exmouth Junction).

Midland Region:
Ivatt 2-6-2 tanks 41309, 41316 (72A Exmouth Junction), 2-6-2 tank 42265 (64A Edinburgh St. Margaret's), 42269 (65A Glasgow Eastfield), Crab 2-6-0 42832 (24F Fleetwood), Ivatt 2-6-0 43123 (51C West Hartlepool), Fowler 4F 0-6-0 44292 (12F Workington), Stanier Black 5 4-6-0 44798 (67A Glasgow Corker Hill), 44921 (63A Perth), 45117 (67B Hurlford), 45497 (67C Ayr), Ivatt 2-6-0 mogul 46482 (67D Ardrossan).

Eastern/North Eastern Region:
Gresley 4-6-2 A3 60037 (64A Edinburgh Haymarket), Peppercorn A2 4-6-2 60530 (64A Edinburgh Haymarket), V2 4-6-0 60972 (61B Kittybrewster), B1 4-6-0 61133 (62A Thornton), 61354 (62A Thornton), 65251 (64F Bathgate).

BR Standards:

Class 5 4-6-0 73064 (66A Glasgow Polmadie), 2-6-0 moguls 76024 (67B Hurlford), 76107 (61B Kittybrewster), 78045 (61B Kittybrewster), 2-6-4 tanks 80030 (67A Glasgow Corker Hill) 80022 (64A Edinburgh Haymarket), WD Austerity 2-8-0 90056 (56B Ardesley), 90571 (50A York), 9F 2-10-0 92034 (40B Immingham), 92149 (34E Peterborough New England).